How To Profit From
DISINFLATION

Myron Simons

NEW CENTURY PUBLISHERS, INC.

Printing Code

11   12   13   14   15   16

Library of Congress Cataloging in Publication Data
Simons, Myron.
    How to profit from disinflation.

    Bibliography: p.
    Includes index.
    1. Investments—United States. 2. Deflation
(Finance)—United States. 3. United States—
Economic conditions—1971-   . I. Title.
II. Title: Disinflation.
HG4921.S55   1982   332.6′78   82-8030
ISBN 0-8329-0146-6   AACR2

To my father

Murray Simons

who taught me more than I know

Contents

Preface

One of the smartest Wall Streeters I knew did most of his investing during recessions. He described it like this: "When the markets are in trouble, the values get to be fantastic. I see so many of them that I hardly know which ones to choose. I sometimes feel like a kid in a candy shop." Later on, when the markets had recovered, his excitement faded away, and he seemed a little bored, just as the rest of us were getting excited. He began coldly to dispose of his candy store goodies to create cash so that he could be ready for the next downturn. It must have been a good technique. After having been virtually penniless in the late 1930s, his fortune totaled over $100 million by the early 1970s.

It's easy to say "do thou likewise." But it's terribly difficult to resist those boom days when the profits seem so easy that we all feel like financial geniuses. Still, that's what must be done if you are going to profit from the present financial crisis—and you must be willing to part with some of your treasures so that you can raise cash, even if they are no longer selling at their highest levels. As Shakespeare said, "Put cash in thy purse." And wait! And then wait some more, until it seems impossible to resist the values you are able to buy. That's when it makes sense to invest. That's when there are opportunities to do much better than to make those risky bucks from a fast temporary bounce. Forget trying to beat inflation by a few percentage points. Instead, you'll have the chance to make many, many times your money.

Of course, I am assuming that the United States will recover from the deep recession that is now here. Our country has been through somewhat similar things before, and there's no reason to think that it can't pull out of it this time. In fact, the prophets of doom are, in my opinion, simply sensationalists like those West Coast crazies of the 1950s who used to proclaim the end of the world regularly, complete with a date for the cataclysm. For a while they received a great deal of attention; but after a number of end-of-the-world dates had passed and we were still here, they became laughing stocks.

So, don't flee from civilization and stock some country cellar with a year's supply of groceries. Just put some cash in a safe investment and stick it out. The process of dis-inflation, which is already surprisingly well on its way to success, will be very painful, and its results will last for quite some time—just as have similiar periods throughout history. But, our economy and the climate for investing will return to a far healthier state than they have been in for a very long time.

This book will begin by attempting to convince you to make a special effort to raise some cash because the current recession will be long and deep. If it succeeds in doing that, it will have accomplished the first part of its job. The second part will work toward helping you to prepare to use that cash to become richer once the economic storm is over.

CHAPTER 1

A Healthy Economy

Can We Get There from Here?

Disinflation is now with us. Prices won't break sharply enough to be called deflation; so a new word, "disinflation," must be coined, just as the term "recession" was created in 1937 by President Roosevelt to indicate that the economy was going to slump again, but not as badly as it did in 1932. Right now, even a modest decline in prices is going to be poisonous for an economy that is as geared to inflation as ours has been. It means that cutting inventories won't be enough to create a fast snap-back; they will stay too lean to cause massive re-ordering until businessmen get adjusted to the fact that everything they buy can't be pushed out of the door at higher prices. Consumers will be much slower to think that they had better buy now because today's bargains won't be available for long. Unemployment will be very high, and companies with tightly stretched credit will fall by the wayside. The banking system must worry about an increasing amount of bad debts.

Call it recession, or depression, it won't be over with until a nasty shake-out has taken place. However, it won't last for a decade, like the Great Depression. We would need something stronger than disinflation to make that happen. It will be bad, and the economic expansion we are all hoping for will have to wait for some time before the slowdown runs its course. But, it will be a wonderful time for those with money to plan and execute investment programs for taking advantage of what the future has to offer.

Ending Inflation

Economists love the story about the frontier woman who came home one day only to see her husband locked in mortal combat with a gigantic grizzly bear. She sized up the situation for a minute or two, and then yelled, "Go it, husband, go it bear!" The tale is usually used as an illustration of how difficult it is to choose between two evils. Perhaps we should take our cue from the frontier woman when we root about inflation. The process of ending it may be so unpleasant that we could wind up cheering "Go it inflation, go it disinflation."

Of course, right now, the cheering sections are very one-sided. There is a virtual worldwide consensus pulling for the end of inflation, even though there may be some economic pain that must be accepted before prices begin to go down. But, let's look at the record! In the last 50 years, the only two periods that have seen prices on the downside for more than one year were in 1929-1933, and 1937-1938. True, there was a small downtick in 1949, but it was more of an interruption in the uptrend than a real change in the price revolution which has been so persistent that even the recessions of the three decades following 1949 could do little more than slow the advance in the thrust of inflation.

In effect, history tells us that if we want to slow inflation, we can. But, we may have to undergo a slump in business more like that of the 1930s than even the most serious downturn since World War II—that of 1974-5 —which still left inflation growing at an unacceptably high rate. We'd better ask ourselves if we really want that!

Of course, nearly everyone agrees that it would be just wonderful to clear away the debris of the past and embark on a new period of economic growth such as that of the 30 years following 1940.

What a blissful change that would be! With a low inflation rate and low interest rates, and far less intervention from the Government, our economy could once again strive toward the goal of steady growth with low unemployment and a higher measure of satisfaction of individual needs. The Federal Reserve could retreat into the background of obscurity in which it functioned so cheerfully until the Arthur Burns era which began in 1969. Businessmen could make long-term plans without worrying about the next credit crunch or Government-induced economic slowdowns. No wonder there's unaminity about reaching that point!

However, that can all turn out to be an Utopian dream. It's a little like the wish to see the Earth and Moon from a cozy viewing point on Mars. It would be wonderful, of course! But getting to the Red Planet is so difficult that for almost everyone it is an impossible dream. Like the fantasy trips to far-off places, economics is seldom wish-fulfilling.

The present position of the United States economy, which lies neatly between a rock and a hard place, was arrived at by a long process of mishandling our domestic affairs and a few tough breaks internationally. It all began when President Johnson refused to ask Congress for a sizeable tax increase to pay for the Vietnam War. His monetary advisers knew better, but the President was skating on thin ice with a Congress that never really intended to authorize as large a struggle as that which occurred in Vietnam. He wasn't about to risk the criticism he would face if he went back to that body. So, instead, he paid for the war by increasing the Federal debt and by persuading the Federal Reserve to buy enough of the newly issued bonds to make it appear like "business as usual." In the process, the Fed pumped reserves into the banking system, which had the same effect as printing billions of dollars of new money. History should have told the President that it couldn't fly. Most of the nasty inflations the world has seen came about precisely from wars that were paid for by debt and the printing of money. So, before the Vietnam War was over, the stage was set for a sharp increase in the underlying inflation rate.

Perhaps President Nixon could have revived our economic structure if he had been willing to accept a typical post-war recession. Instead, he chose to go the route of price controls, which merely postponed the inevitable. The controls and their ultimate end caused a tremendous build-up of inventories. Easing out of them, more than anything else, was responsible for the recession of 1974–5. At first, that recession looked deep enough to ease inflation, but President Ford wasn't willing to face the consequences and muffed the best opportunity in years to end the upward price cycle. We came out of the deepest recession in the post-World War II period without anything to show for it.

Even that amount of Government misdirection might not have damaged the powerful United States economy if it hadn't been for OPEC, which led the way to higher inflation and lower productivity throughout the entire industrialized world. Once again, the energy policy of the United States couldn't measure up to the needs, so we came out of our hardship with little to show for it. No one should be enchanted with the present comfortable position, since it seems more due to the worldwide recession than anything intelligent on our part.

It's no surprise that the voters decided by a landslide that they wanted something different. Ronald Reagan promised to change our direction. His ideas, in general, involve a step backward to the simpler time of less Government intervention.

1. Give the Federal Government a stronger hand in dealing with its traditional role of the defender of the nation by increasing its military posture.

2. Take the money for military spending away from the wildly expanding social services.

3. Encourage private industry to take over future expansion efforts by giving it tax incentives.

4. Make certain that any dislocations in the economy caused by the switch in emphasis from the government to

the private sector will be cured by increased consumer spending. A phased-in tax reduction, theoretically, will accomplish that. The plan has the virtue of being the tried-and-true method by which every recession in the post-war has been ended—except that Reagan's plan starts out with the appearance of being less Keynsian because of its deemphasis of Federal spending on everything but the military.

5. By some sort of magic, balance the budget so that interest rates will decline to a level that will promote rather than discourage business expansion. (That idea has already been thrown out of the window, as the deficits in President Reagan's proposed budget have reached record levels.)

6. Naturally, this program of so-called "supply-side" economics is expected to increase production while monetary expansion remains modest. That should bring inflation under control and reduce the need of labor for extraordinary wage increases and cost-of-living benefits such as those it has been receiving for the last decade.

It's a program that sounds reasonable enough. If it works, it can put us in the position in which we'd like to find ourselves, and lead the way to a healthy economic expansion. The trouble is that we may not be able to get there from here. The economic pangs we will have to suffer may be so great that the gradual return to health may have to be abandoned in favor of pain-killers.

CHAPTER 2

The Incredible Presidential

Balancing Act

So far, only one part of President Reagan's program has failed. But, it threatens to pull down much of the rest of it. The failure is that there's no chance of getting the budget into balance, or anywhere near it, either this year, or for many years. The only way to make any serious reduction in the flow of red ink is to raise taxes. While any tax increases could be confined to only a handful of products, such as liquor, tobacco, or natural gas, they would take money away from the consumer and reduce some of the benefits that are supposed to flow from the Reagan program. Besides, even if the President decides to agree to higher taxes, Congress is likely to take one good look at the unemployment figures and decide to trade any increases for keeping social programs on stream. Deficits in times of recession, after all, have never frightened politicians in modern times.

How important is budget balancing? Ordinarily, it wouldn't make many waves. But, a near-balanced budget and lower inflation rates are the very key to the success of the efforts of the Federal Reserve Board. That combination would allow a restrained growth in the money supply *and* a push toward lower interest rates. Lower interest rates are essential to give backbone to the economy, at least until the tax reductions provide businessmen and consumers with a reason to increase their spending. There is unquestionably a large pent-up demand for housing and autos, but high interest rates are poison for both industries. It's no wonder that the financial community suffers shock waves at the mere suggestion that there might be little or no decrease in interest rates.

That puts the entire economic game plan into an unpleasant dilemma. On the one hand, if the economic decline slows, or if some mild improvement is seen, the demand for money by the consumer, businessmen, *and* the Treasury will push interest rates up. We've already had plenty of experience with what that can do to our economy. Chances are that it will mean that any mild improvement will be aborted before it has a chance to get started. A double-dip recession could really send the financial markets into a tizzy and force a change in the entire Reagan program.

On the other hand, if the economy doesn't stage any sort of recovery, interest rates can come down. But the downturn will be so severe by that time that any efforts to save the economy will have to be much more heroic than the tax cut which is already in place.

Add it all up and it's apparent that we face a "heads we lose, tails we lose" situation. The only salvation is a change in policy either by the Reagan Administration or the Federal Reserve Board. Since both of them are working on the basis of rigid theories, rather than pragmatic flexibility, a reversal of their stances is a great deal to ask. After all, both are convinced that their programs will take time to work and that following through with them is the only way to bring this country back to economic health. Having too much faith in economic theories is as dangerous as having too much faith in the old-time medicine of blood-letting. They can ignore the present facts in favor of future promises. Economic reality tends to be much too complex for that.

Ever since World War II we have managed to avoid that sickening crunch which happened in past generations, when downturns induced further downturns until the economy was flat on its back. Administration after Administration has rescued us from those accumulating downtrends by short-term pragmatic methods. Even the 1974–5 recession was remedied as quickly as possible. It became as nasty as it did only because President Ford missed his cues and spent the first part of the downturn fighting inflation rather than the plunge in the economy. But, if President Reagan continues to operate with theory rather than pragmatism, *this* downturn has every chance of becoming cumulative.

Changing the game plan may be in the cards, regardless of the Administration's wishes. The Democrats aren't likely to sit still as unemployment grows and interest rates remain sky-high. They will be making moves to undo many of the "supply-side" reforms. But that is likely to leave us with a thoroughly divided Congress. Some Democrats will talk tough, but act gently as they secretly hope that the Republicans will be tarred with the recession brush by the time of the November elections. On the other hand, Conservatives and Republicans will want to continue with the existing theories. This kind of schism brings back unpleasant memories of the Hoover Presidency.

Is the outlook completely without hope? Perhaps not— provided the economy walks on a razor-thin line! There is a possibility that the decline in the inflation rate will allow the Fed to proclaim victory and shift to an easier course. That has a very high degree of probability. The fundamental mainsprings of the inflationary push of the 1970s are almost entirely unraveled. Increasing the money supply somewhat should not rewarm the inflationary trend provided the Fed doesn't become wild, as it has on occasion. If we are lucky, short-term demands for credit can ease and allow the Fed to bring interest rates back to something near their traditional relationship to the inflation rate, which would cause a large drop, especially in long-term rates. That would solve a major problem, but unfortunately, it would leave the economy with many other problems to contend with before it can breathe easier.

Potential Problems

The most important of the potentials for future disaster is the banking system of the world, which is in deep trouble. Thus far, it has managed to disguise its problems by putting them aside. But if the recession continues for much longer, it will probably not be able to continue to do that. The technique that the banks have been using would be comical, if there weren't such serious implications. It is this: if a borrower is important enough, and can't meet his repayment schedule, don't be nasty about it. Above all, don't write off the loan! Simply give him more time to repay the principal, and lend him enough money to keep his interest payments current. That's not quite as silly as it sounds. After all, if a debtor is plunged into bankruptcy, the courts appoint a new management which is likely to be less experienced and less effective than the incumbents. It's better to leave the present group in control and hope that a resurgent economy will allow it to bail out the lenders. Besides, and perhaps most important, doing it that way allows the banks to keep from having to recognize a bad-debt loss. The unhappy fact is that there are now billions of dollars of bad corporate debts that should be charged off the capital of the banks, but are being kept alive instead.

That's only the beginning! The permissiveness toward corporate debt pales in significance compared to that extended toward foreign Government debt. The Polish loans have uncovered reasons for money-center bankers to grow grey hair. Try as they might to accommodate Poland, the situation in that country has deteriorated so much that it's even difficult to apply the usual cosmetic effect of keeping interest payments current and forgetting about the repayment schedule. In the case of Foreign Governments, as with corporate borrowers, it doesn't make much sense to declare insolvency. The assets that could be sequestered would barely make a dent in the amount of credit outstanding. So, for the banks, it's much more important to find a method in which to carry the loans at face value, no matter how ridiculous it seems. Because if the banks, especially some in Austria and Germany, must take substantial reserves against the loans, their capital could be severely damaged. True, central banks can keep their countries from facing old-fashioned panics on the part of depositors. But, Poland is only a small part of the total problem.

For the United States banking system, Poland is of only moderate concern. Argentina is far more significant, since it owes our banks over $9 billion of its total foreign debt of $34 billion. Besides, the dramatic change in the credit worthiness of that asset-rich country simply emphasizes the fragility of the huge foreign loans that the banking system of the world has made to dozens of countries that can be forced into near-default by unexpected events. The money center banks of the United States are reported to have loaned something like twice their combined capital to the non-oil producing less-developed countries. Most of the loans are almost as impossible to collect as is that of Poland. So, a true appraisal of their value would really unveil a nightmare so nasty, that even the Fed might find it difficult to save the banks, as it did some years ago in the isolated case of the Franklin National.

Add to the problems of the money-center banks the more publicized one of the savings banks. A surprising number of them have been suffering losses large enough to threaten their survival. There are two reasons for the difficulties that so many of them face. First, they have been lending money, largely for mortgages, for a number of years. Naturally, they did so at interest rates which were considerably lower than today's. They hold about $350 billion worth of mortgages with interest rates of less than 10%. But now, they have to pay more than the rates at which they made their loans. No wonder they are under such strain! Almost as bad are Federal regulations which keep them from paying competitive interest rates. So, in addition to the negative spread on interest rates, they are suffering from very large-scale withdrawals.

So far, the Federal Deposit Insurance Corporation has been able to rescue the weaker banks. It has forced takeovers of these weaker banks by the stronger ones and, as an incentive, it has guaranteed to make up for some of the more obvious future losses. But, unless interest rates break sharply, a number of other banks will need rescuing.

Of course, it's possible that the banks will get away with it. Putting matters aside can continue indefinitely, as can pushing the weak sisters into stronger hands. But, incredible as it may seem in view of all of the precautions that have been taken, the odds for a slip-up are uncomfortably high. Remember that most of history's economic disasters have been triggered off by a financial crisis!

It would be nice to stop being a Cassandra right here. The potentials for nastiness are already scary enough. But, there are no less than six more problems!

1. Real estate values have risen so tremendously since 1975 that they now account for most of the net worth of the average American family. No wonder our consumers have such a feeling of comfort! Their major asset has tripled or quadrupled, and made them richer than they had ever hoped. What's more, our financial system has followed along with the advance. Mortgages were increased, and there's a large complex of second mortgages and so-called "creative financial instruments." It has allowed the American family to have the cash to cope with inflation without cutting back on consumption. Let's hope that real estate values don't plunge, as they have so often in the past. Because, if they retreat to the levels of three or four years ago, it will cause a number of financial problems and it may put a big enough dent in consumer confidence to more than offset the benefits from any tax cut. As long as interest rates remain high, the probability of a slide in the real estate market is uncomfortably high.

2. Farm income isn't nearly as important as it was during the 1930s, when President Roosevelt made it one of the priorities for overcoming the Depression. But, it is still important enough to be a factor in our economic well-being. Like many things, there's a two-edged aspect to farm income. Lower food prices are a major element in reducing inflation, so the farmer's problems have been taken rather lightly. Of course, bumper crops have accounted for some of the decline in prices, and that usually keeps farm income growing. But, the modern farm is highly mechanized, and that means heavy debt. What's more, high energy prices

have cut into profits for some time. With interest rates as high as they are, farmers are finding it almost impossible to make ends meet. It's not going to be easy for them to buy new equipment or to maintain the value of their land holdings.

3. One of the most significant changes in the post-War period has been the rapid growth in spending by State and Local governments. By now they account for close to 40% of overall Government spending. Somehow, taxpayers grumble a great deal about Federal taxes, but their strongest outrage is reserved for local taxes. So there have been a number of cutbacks on local levels. That's just the beginning. The Reagan program is going to cause further substantial cuts in local government spending. In fact, a number of states and municipalities are calling for higher taxes, which might offset some of the benefits of Federal tax cuts. For the first time in many years, overall Government employment will be going down just as unemployment in the private sector is rising.

4. Increased capital spending is one of the underpinnings of the Reagan economic plan. But, there's no indication that businessmen are willing to invest in new plants and equipment until there's a clearer view of the economic future. After all, with inflation coming down and interest rates high, there's good reason to wait. Tax benefits are likely to persuade them to go forward some day, but not until they are sure that they can sell the products generated by new capacity. So long as capacity utilization is close to the lowest levels of the post-War period, any resurgence of capital spending is improbable. In fact, the largest bulge is coming from the oil companies, and since the lion's share is for exploration, it has smaller economic effect than other basic industry expansion. Not much help can be expected from this quarter for some time.

5. Consumer spending is weakening. The only time it picks up is when merchandise is sold at a considerable discount. There's still a hangover from deeply ingrained inflationary expectations. The idea that a bargain should be snapped up before prices rise again has persuaded consumers to keep buying on the cuff, even if they can't really

afford it. Of course, widespread discounting creates a problem for retailers. Since profit margins are small, it's not such a good idea to carry large inventories and to pay high interest rates in order to do so. So, even though there has been some inventory cutting, we may not be in for any rebuilding. Besides, both consumers and merchants are likely to change their attitudes about jumping at price reductions once they are convinced that the inflation rate is actually declining rapidly.

6. World trade is already down, and it threatens to take a deeper plunge. Europe is in a deepening recession. But the biggest drawback is the apparent financial suicide of allowing less-developed and Eastern European countries to buy on credit. That's just throwing good money after bad. The dilemma is that those countries were very good customers. It will make a considerable dent in industrial production to cut them off. It comes at a time when unemployment in Europe is already higher than it has been since the Great Depression.

Fortunately, there are some potentially favorable factors to offset all of the gloom and doom. They are the things that keep so many economists hoping for a relatively early end to the recession.

1. Our economy has changed from one in which basic industry was dominant to one in which service industries lead the way. Thus far, the service industries have kept expanding, even in past recessions. Almost 73% of non-farm employment is now accounted for by service industries, up from under 60% in the early 1950s. They are less dependent than basic industry on interest rates, and they have a chance of remaining relatively immune from the present downturn. But, it is difficult to estimate the probability that spending for social services will stay high if inflationary expectations diminish.

2. There's a huge pent-up demand for autos and housing. If interest rates *can* be lowered, those industries can lead the way to recovery, just as they led the downturn.

3. Consumer spending has rescued every post-War re-

cession. More money is jangling in the average American's pocketbook. If it is spent the downturn should be over.

4. Defense spending will rise more than 18% this year, and it will be gaining in momentum later in the year. Heavy defense spending has rescued us from more than one recession. But, it's a good idea to look beyond the bare figures. This round of defense spending will lay more emphasis on highly sophisticated, very expensive weapons. It will make less of a dent in unemployment than at any time in the past.

It seems like an uncomfortably small group of positive factors to face up to such an array of negatives, doesn't it? That doesn't mean that they *can't* win out. They can, although the odds are against it. But, for a number of months it's going to be like walking on a tightrope over a pool filled with hungry man-eating sharks. It's a period that may go down in history as President Reagan's incredible balancing act.

CHAPTER 3

The Inflationary Cycle Is Over

With all of the problems that our economy faces, it's absolutely astonishing that so few people ask what will happen when the inflationary push comes to a halt. The fact is that there isn't *any* upward momentum left. The figures since the beginning of 1982 show a mild advance, but that's because they are misleading. For example, housing prices, according to the Retail Price Index, are still on the rise. Actually, they are not! It is difficult to obtain a survey of the true selling prices of homes, but most of us know that the dollar figures are misleading. Existing homes are being sold for significantly under the asking prices, which are still pegged to the sales that took place in mid-1981. Even when they are sold for those high prices, it's usually because discounts are offered in the form of mortgages far below the going rates.

What's more, most retail merchants are selling everything from ready-to-wear clothes to automobiles at sharp discounts, which are not picked up by the reported price index figures. The price of oil is lower and food prices are relatively stable. It all adds up to this—if the data released by Government agencies actually reflected the real prices for buyers, the inflation rate would be negative rather than slightly higher.

In spite of this, very few of our so-called experts are willing to take the present figures seriously. Part of the reason is that they have seen it all before. Inflation has usually yielded to previous recessions, but it has always returned with greater force. Administration after Administration has struggled with inflation ever since World War II, always with some short-lived success, but never with any long-term effect.

The continual ebb and flow in the struggle against inflation has finally convinced most of those who are interested in financial matters that it is wise to invest whenever prices give some ground and to sell only when a new fight against inflation begins, even though this time it's likely to be quite different. Let's look at the record.

Believe it or not, President Eisenhower began to worry about inflation way back in 1958. He stood by cheering while the Federal Reserve raised interest rates. By today's standards, the rates seem very low. But, when the commercial paper rate went up almost 14% from 3.6% to 4.1%, it helped to trigger off the recession of 1958. It wasn't a terribly deep one, but it was enough to elect Kennedy by a narrow margin, a fact that Richard Nixon never forgot in tailoring his economic plans to fit the needs of election years. Since the fight was abandoned, it never did much to end inflation completely, even though the rate during the late 1950s would have appeared as a god send for the last few years. About the only good it did was to unearth some wonderful investment opportunities—something that the end of all of the fights against inflation had in common.

President Kennedy also had his tussle with inflation. It led him to an attack on the steel companies and a rather nasty rollback of the price increases that they had attempted to impose. The investment community didn't care for that at all, and the stock market plunged into one of the sharpest declines that had been seen since the 1930s. It took a while to recover, but soon everyone in Washington had forgotten about the inflation and began to concentrate on the Kennedy assasination and then on Vietnam. Once again, the struggle was abandoned, and once again the profit potential for common stocks and almost any other kind of investible was extraordinary—at least until the next fight against inflation began.

It was President Johnson who oversaw the next one. He had reason to worry about inflation! The Vietnam War was costing far more than he had expected. He not only had no desire to pay the freight, but he feared that Congress would seize any attempt to raise taxes for the continuation of the struggle to unleash violent opposition, and perhaps a re-examination of the Gulf of Tonkin resolution on which he based the escalation of the War. So, he called in the Federal Reserve and the result was the first of our so-called credit crunches. But, it was soon called off and, as usual, we had wonderful days for investment that didn't end until President Nixon was elected.

As one of his top priorities, President Nixon promised to end inflation. He certainly tried! The first attempt came in the form of another credit crunch, this one officiated by the Federal Reserve's new Chairman, Dr. Arthur Burns. Investibles fell sharply, along with the stock market. Once again, when the fight was abandoned in 1970, the time to re-invest had come.

President Ford reached office at an unusually difficult time. Not only was the nation in a state of political shock because of the forced resignation of President Nixon, but inflation once more seemed a terrible problem. In spite of the fact that a severe recession was lurking, President Ford acted on the advice of the top economists in America, whom he assembled in a rare publicly televised session. They told him to fight inflation. So he issued his famous WIN (Whip Inflation Now) buttons and the market for investibles simply plunged. It all ended in the 1974-5 recession, the deepest in post-War history. But, when the concern had switched from inflation to recession fighting, it was the best time in years to invest in almost any form of stock, real estate, or collectible.

The conclusion is obvious: every recent President has had his struggle with inflation. Investors have always suffered severly during those struggles, but once they were over, anyone who was ready to put up their money benefitted tremendously. So, when the fight against inflation begins, get into cash or short-term investments. Keep a tight grip on those liquid assets until the fight is over, and then invest as heavily as you can. No wonder 1982s buyers are ready to jump the gun and assume that President Reagan's fight against inflation will soon be over. But the difference this time around is that inflation won't be coming back with its usual rush. Investors had better be more careful about their timing this time because if disinflation is the order of the day it could be wise to wait to see just how far down the economy can plunge before deciding to reinvest.

Despite the signals that the inflation rate is declining, it's likely to be a while before the economic fraternity and the public are willing to believe it. After all, with a history of higher prices extending persistently over two decades, it's much easier to think that the current tough anti-inflation policy will be softened. If so, the reasoning goes, the economy will come roaring back, and prices will start to rise again. Most economists still work on the Newtonian principle that objects move in a straight line unless they are met by a sufficiently large off-setting force. For years now, that force has been enough monetary restraint to lead to recession. Once it is over, the path of inflation has always continued to rise, so there's an inclination to believe that there won't be any change in the pattern this time. However, that kind of reasoning ignores one other basic principle: once the underlying momentum is lost, a resumption of the upward push is no longer probable. That's what seems to be happening right now. Even so, those economists who see those strong signals flashing find it very hard to resist the temptation to say only pleasant things. Remember that even Herbert Hoover kept insisting that prosperity was just around the corner, while that the economy was sinking into its morass.

Why the Top Economists Sing Us Lullabies

Maybe it's true that the only things that are inevitable are death and taxes. Still, there are many events that are so probable that they are rather close to inevitable. So, it's surprising that the economists, who are supposed to warn us about the nastiness that is still to come, are lulling us to sleep with talk of a near-by business recovery. It may seem a bit conceited to fly in the face of all those experts, both in private life and in government—at least until you take a good hard look at how even the best of them work. They find it very hard to rock the boat in their public statements.

Behind the scenes, most economists are in a state of confusion and change their forecasts with even more than the usual speed as the economy shows trends that are contradictory to what should be happening. A good example is that it has been terribly difficult to get a fix where interest rates are going. Even more confusing has been the ability of businessmen and the banking system to cope with record breaking rates for as long as they have. Most economists were proven wrong in the Spring of 1980 when they were so concerned that the extraordinary plunge of the second quarter of 1980 would continue to do severe damage. So, when interest rates set a new high in the early Fall of 1981, the majority expressed only mild feelings of alarm. They haven't budged from that conclusion, partly because Reaganomics is still a strange and attractive beast, and they would like to play it close to the vest. After all, they would lose much of their creditability if they blow their forecasts again so soon after the last time.

It's clear that economists, in general, prefer gradual and moderate change. That's when their undoubtedly good educations and their computers can detect the ins and outs of the business scene. But they ignore two historical facts. First, high interest rates take some time before they have their full effect, and for a long while there is a temptation to think that any deterioration can be easily reversed and is therefore temporary. Second, sharp downturns in business that are too complicated to reverse easily usually hit with sudden fierceness, in contrast to the climb toward prosperity, which tends to take a slower and more foreseeable course. In 1982, the record high interest rates are not the only problem, unlike other times when a reversal in rates was able to pull the economies of the world out of their tailspins. This time, they are piled on top of a number of equally severe problems.

There have been economists who have been able to predict sudden changes in business conditions. The most noteworthy was John Maynard Keynes, who is currently in disrepute because his theories, which helped so much in softening the depression of the 1930s, were used too long and in an exaggerated way. But he was able to prove his skill in one of the most dramatic displays of forecasting in economic history.

The Scene: The palace of Versailles, a remembrance of the glory of Imperial France.

The Plot: To extract revenge from Germany for the destruction incurred during World War I.

The Cast: Principal Actors Georges Clemenceau of France, Lloyd George of England, and Woodrow Wilson of the United States. Supporting them was a cast of hundreds, including economists, politicians, and other experts.

The Play: Here at Versailles, a horrible political and economic mistake was made. So anxious were Clemenceau and Lloyd George to show how tough they could be toward Germany, that they power-housed a far gentler and wiser Woodrow Wilson, and wound up by imposing reparation payments that led to the incredible German inflation of 1923. In the fairly traceable line, the course of events then plunged Germany into a mare's nest of economic discontent, the disenchantment of the middle class, and eventually to Adolph Hitler.

One economic expert, John Maynard Keynes, representing England, protested loudly. When he couldn't get the attention of the leaders, he resigned his position and wrote a book entitled *The Economic Consequences of the Peace*, in which he predicted a great many of the events that were to follow. Naturally, the book didn't win him any popularity contests. But it still stands as perhaps the leading example of the ability to make economic predictions by combining a bit of courage with a lot of knowledge.

Unfortunately, there doesn't seem to be anyone like Keynes among today's leading economists. In fact, all too many of the present group work in the same way as weathermen before information sources such as satellite photographs and computer forecasts became available. Remember those days? Meteorologists would get their surface weather maps from reports of pressure, temperature, and cloud cover; then, they would simply move the main weather patterns in the appropriate direction and at the indicated speed and make their forecasts accordingly. Naturally, they were often wrong. The technique of forecasting gradual change worked fine when nothing important was about to errupt. But, whenever anything big and new was about to happen, they missed it.

Still, World War II meteorologists, like today's economists, became so confident of their extrapolating abilities that they often risked the lives of inexperienced pilots unnecessarily. In order to get them to become more critical of their own forecasts, some of the older hands in Air Force meteorology began to circulate an embarrassing (and perhaps apocryphal) story. It seems that an infantry private walked into a weather station on the Gulf Coast of the United States and asked about the forecast for the next day. From his Southern drawl, it was obvious that he had grown up in the area. When the meteorologist in charge told him that it would be fair and sunny, he shook his head and said, "There's going to be a hurricane." Asked why he thought so, he could only reply that the air smelt that way. Of course, you can guess what happened. The official forecast went out "Fair and Sunny" and the hurricane came in right on the soldier's schedule. But, even after that story, meteorologists kept right on moving their weather patterns across the map and making their forecasts without considering the possibility of a dramatic change.

Economists do just about the same thing. They establish the present economic patterns and then they move them up or down a bit in what they think is the right direction and speed. That way, they'll do a satisfactory job most of the time. But, they'll miss the hurricanes. Unfortunately, catching the big blows is what we really need them for.

Perhaps that explains why the majority of businessmen polled recently said that they pay little attention to the economic services to which they subscribe, even though they are very expensive. After all, businessmen must make their plans on a long-term basis. A new plant may take several years to build, and new products or corporate strategies can take even longer to take hold. So, they really can't peg their futures to the vacillations of the economists. Why do they keep paying for the services? Because they get a flow of information that can guide them in the near term and because they feel that they need to touch all bases before making decisions.

That's exactly how all of us should use the economists we read about or subscribe to. They are very good at unearthing the facts we need to form our own conclusions. It's too bad for all of us that their work can't be more imaginative. Because, if it were, it might help our politicians avoid some of the problems that lie ahead. But, with a bunch of hurricane-missers on the job, how can we hope that anyone in charge will batten down the hatches?

Those Misleading Economic Statistics

In the second quarter of 1980, the statistics reported that the economy plunged at a rate which rivaled some of the quarters of the 1930s. Yet, except for autos and housing and some related industries, few of us felt any pain. Then in the first quarter of 1981, the data showed a rate of growth which said "Happy Days are Here Again." But no one felt particularly prosperous. In fact, autos and housing were still suffering badly and most of our politicians were talking about what we would have to do to recover from the recession. How can we make any sense out of these apparent contradictions?

Statistics represent only a sampling of reality. So, it's not unusual that they can be misleading if they are taken too literally. That's particularly true of our modern economy, which is no longer made up of mostly blue collar workers and basic industry.

The economy of the United States is now made up of five sectors, many of which have divergent trends. Defense, for instance, won't have the same pattern as autos or housing. Neither will the service industries or the rapidly growing health care sector. Under the circumstances, it's a good idea to use the economic data as a guideline, but adjust them to conform to the larger reality.

Looking back to early 1980 can help us to shed some light on the subject. The Fed had tightened interest rates in late 1979, but the economy resisted fairly well. Then came the Soviet invasion of Afghanistan, coupled with a worsening situation in Iran. The international markets ran wild. Gold soared to nearly $900 an ounce and carried other metals and commodities with it. Fearful of a terrible burst of inflation, President Carter held a series of budget tightening conferences, which turned out to be fruitless. And the Fed stepped down very hard on the monetary brakes. It even went so far as to call on the banks to limit consumer lending and the use of credit cards. Temporarily, those actions dried up consumer purchasing and pushed basic industry downward sharply. The economic data, which are principally intended to measure those very sectors, responded with a real fainting spell.

However, other sectors of the economy didn't have time to feel the pinch. And, the Fed relented in great haste, fearing the destruction it could cause. Interest rates plunged and credit cards came back out of hiding. Above all, inflationary expectations remained undimished. So, the consumer began to spend again and the economy recovered in a seemingly magical way. Actually, what had happened was that a temporary period of restraint had caused the artificial slowdown and as soon as the pressure was lifted, the economy bounced back to normal.

After President Reagan won the election by a landslide, there was an increased feeling of optimism in business circles. That had its effect in early 1981. Once again, inflationary expectations remained high and caused the consumer to respond, especially to discount sales. And, once again, the economic data were artificially pushed upward.

So, we had two quarters of exaggeration, one on the negative side, the other on the plus side. If we adjust both of them and smooth out the curve of economic growth, we obtain a sensible reading of what actually happened. We have been through a prolonged period of very sluggish growth—one in which some sectors of our business community can claim good times, while others have been experiencing disaster, and most have had a rather flat growth curve. That's been occurring for approximately two years.

Usually, such a stagnant period is the springboard for a substantial move, and it's easy for those with rose-colored glasses to assume that it will be an upward one. That's especially true because even in the period of stagnation, we had a high degree of inflation and the feeling that it would continue in a modified form, even though it might decline some from time to time. Throughout history, such inflationary expectations have been good for business, even though everyone complains a great deal. Economic activity remains high because everyone is convinced that if you don't buy now, you'll have to pay higher prices in the future.

But, what happens if inflation is really over? The fact that business has remained so sluggish even in the face of inflation is a strong indication that there is real trouble brewing. When inflation subsides, the main prop holding up the economy will be knocked out. That's exactly what the economic data show, once we smooth out the bumpy curve. The odds are very firmly in favor of a continued disinflation and a prolonged sharp downturn in business activity.

DISCHARM—Key Signals That Inflation Is Over

In order to lower inflationary expectations, the Government must create a certain amount of disenchantment. It must convince the majority in all walks of life that the price level will not continue to soar. That kind of disenchantment takes some doing, because it is also so politically expedient to talk about prosperity being just around the corner. So, it takes more time to get the idea across than it does for many other, much less complicated political economic concepts.

Disenchantment is too long a word to use as a puzzle solver. But, since enchantment is a kind of charm, I have butchered the English language a bit to make the requirement of the Reagan Administration to DISCHARM the public about inflation. There's an ulterior motive in this newly coined word. It helps me to remember the first letters of the signals to watch for if I want an early warning of whether inflation is likely to end or to return.

D stands for Dollar. The greenback is volatile, but it's easy to track, since the currency figures are quoted every day in the financial newspapers. Its movements are an indication of what the rest of the world, including the gnomes of Switzerland, think about our inflation rate versus the rest of the world. It's also a reflection of our interest rates. There's a large amount of so-called "hot money" that flips around the world looking for the best short-term return. But, the dollar is the base currency for the entire Western world, and we *do* have the most stable government in the world. So, when the dollar suffers any appreciable weakness, it is a clear prediction that our inflation rate will be high. Recently, the dollar has been almost too strong. Its continuing upward trend is an indication that the wily money traders are optimistic about our ability to bring down the inflation rate. What's more, the very strength of the greenback enables us to buy everything from the rest of the world at lower real prices, an anti-inflation factor in itself.

I is for Interest rates. Many kinds of interest-bearing instruments are traded in large volume every day, so their rise or fall is easy to track. As a forecaster of the future inflation rate, the price of long-term bonds of the highest quality is of particular significance. There's an old rule of thumb that says that long-term Treasuries should yield 2–3% more than the inflation rate. Recently, even though inflation has been abating, bonds have been yielding much more than that, because of the general feeling that prices will begin to rise again once the economy improves. The very large spread between long-term bond prices and the most recent inflation rate, which has been running at under 3% for some months, is a vote of no-confidence in our ability to keep inflation down for very long. But, if there's any increased indication that business will continue to do badly for a prolonged period of time you can be sure that long-term bond interest rates will drop sharply.

Short-term rates differ from long-term rates in that they are more dependent on supply–demand and Federal Reserve policy than anything else. Guesses about the future of inflation are probably the most important single element of the Fed's decision making. But, since that body is pledged to control the rate of increase of the money supply rather than interest rates, it has other considerations to work with, especially in the short term. While it is important to keep watching for trends in Federal funds, and in Treasury Bills, they are a less important signal for determining the bond market's opinion of the future of inflation than long-term rates. Until those rates get closer to that of the most recent inflation numbers, they will indicate a continuation of inflationary expectations.

S stands for the Sales–inventory ratio. This indicator should move in exactly the opposite direction to inflation. As it rises, inflationary expectations should fall and vice versa. The figure is reported monthly, so it should be easy to track. If it starts to shrink back toward an inventory total of 1.4 months worth of sales, it would indicate a need for business to keep ordering merchandise at a high level. On the other hand, if it stays at 1.5 months worth of sales, or more, it indicates a need for inventory cutting, leading to a back-up in the pipelines that keep our manufacturers going. What's more, if merchants aren't moving enough inventory, we should see a lot of discount sales, pushing the price level downward.

C is for Commodity prices. They are a sensitive forecaster of the future price level, and they are easy to follow in the financial press. Naturally, some commodities are subject to weather and other natural phenomena. So it is important to watch the general trend rather than any short-term move in a small selected group of items.

Precious metals are also important. We've heard so much about gold in the last few years that it has become a symbol of safety and protection from political turmoil. But, it is a commodity and anything that undermines inflationary expectations also puts a dent in the price of gold. In fact, whenever the Federal Reserve shows determination to tighten, watch gold decline along with most other commodities.

Ever since the sharp bulge after the Soviet invasion of Afghanistan, commodities have been in a long downtrend. That's a far cry from other periods of business slowdown during the 1970s, when raw material and energy prices kept mounting with only brief interruptions. It gives good reason to hope that even a resumption of moderate economic growth will not bring inflation roaring back.

H is for Home prices. Even when housing starts have been in a depression, the price of new homes has been stable or even rising. That is largely a reflection of the fact that costs have been going up even though business hasn't been good. But prices of existing homes are related to inflationary expectations more than almost any other single factor in our economy. The reason is that a house or cooperative apartment represents the largest investment made by the average family. The escalation in the value over the last four years has made most homeowners *feel* rich even if they have no intention of selling. Until recently, many householders have actually increased their mortgages to keep up with their spending patterns. Should the bubble burst, the feeling of prosperity will fade along with it. There is no single element that will end inflationary expectations faster than a decline in the value of existing homes. This is an indicator that is somewhat more difficult to track than most of the others because it isn't reported in many newspapers. What's more, there are a great many ways to give discounts on houses, such as the granting of mortgages for below the existing market, that will not appear in any report.

Prices for existing homes have begun to decline, although the decrease is still of modest proportions. It will take a sharper break before home owners become alarmed. But, that is a distinct possibility.

A is for Art and antique auctions. When auction prices fly wildly higher, as they did during the previous three years, it means that a great deal of money is being spent by people who think that collectibles will appreciate considerably against the dollar. Since auction buyers and sellers tend to be somewhat aware of world conditions, it's worth considering their opinions. Auction prices aren't as widely reported as other economic data, but the New York *Times* reports on auctions in its Friday edition. *Christie's Auction Gallery* publishes a letter on auction events, and *Art and Auction Magazine* is another source of information.

Recently there has been a gradual deterioration in the prices of all but the most desireable objects, which are the province of the extremely rich. It's another sign that inflationary expectations have lost their force.

R is for Retail sales. They are reported soon after the end of each month. Unfortunately, one of the unpleasant facts of economic life that the Reagan Administration must face is that anything that dampens inflation will also put a crimp in retail sales. Consumer spending has the main factor in ending every recession since World War II. In fact, the tax cut of Reaganomics is expected to increase consumption in late 1982. But, there is some question whether lower taxes will have the desired effect if inflation is no longer a cause for buyer eagerness.

Department store and other retail sales are staying at a high level only because of deep discounting, even of quality merchandise. That has cut into profit margins and caused merchants to hesitate before reordering. The discounting won't show up in the Government's economic data. But, of course, any real trend toward price-cutting is just what inflation fighters are looking for.

M stands for Money supply. With the growing popularity of the monetarist theory, the money supply has taken on greater significance as an indication of future inflation. It makes a great deal of sense. If the money supply increases too rapidly, there is likely to be the classic situation in which too many dollars are chasing the same amount of goods and services. Hence, higher prices will be paid. But, as the Fed warns, these money supply increases must continue for months before they have any effect. The attention paid to week-by-week movements is greatly overdone by Wall Street.

Of course, the best of possible worlds is one in which interest rates decline without causing the money supply to rise rapidly. In fact, that's usually what happens in a recession, when lower demand for loans keeps interest rates on the down side even without an increase in banking funds. On the other hand, the worst of possible worlds is one in which the money supply keeps rising even with very high interest rates. The Fed got into that dilemma late in 1981 and early 1982. In that case, what happened was that the Treasury's demand for money was huge and businessmen, in order to carry inventories that weren't moving, kept right on borrowing.

When inflation is over, both the money supply and interest rates decline. That seemed about to happen in the Fall of 1981, but it was completely reversed when winter arrived. Both are still too high, and that may help to push business activity down, but it's by no means an indication of lower inflation.

Keeping track of the money supply can turn out to be very complex. The trouble is that there are too many ways of measuring it. The Federal Reserve publishes data on a variety of measurements, which it refers to as M's. M-1 (a bundling of the old M-1A and M-1B) includes checking accounts, both noninterest and interest bearing, and currency in circulation. And then, there are also M-2, and M-3, each including more data. It all culminates with "L", which includes everything, including the financial kitchen sink. So, some economists have decided to cut through all of the confusion by basing their judgments on the monetary base, another figure reported weekly by both Washington and the Federal Reserve Bank of St. Louis.

The trouble with all this wealth of data is that each measurement gives a different indication. The old M-1A, the least inclusive, showed the smallest growth in 1980. It grew at a 4.2% rate. Each time there were more data included, the rate went up a bit, until it reached 10.1% by the time it reached M-3. The alternative, the monetary base, increased by 8.2%. Those increases had to be reduced, according to the monetarist theory, if inflation rates were to decline.

The scorecard of DISCHARM shows that everything is pointed toward disinflation, except for the two sister indicators of money supply and interest rates. Fortunately, they can change most rapidly. In fact, with the business decline likely to continue, and perhaps deepen, it seems only a question of time until they join with the other mainsprings of inflation in pointing unanimously downward. That hasn't happened since inflation became a serious problem in the early 1970s. Even in the recessions, there were a number of raw material and energy prices pointing upward.

Of course, the monthly Consumer Price Index may push up and down because of external events, such as terrible winter weather, which can temporarily push food prices up, or because of a sudden decline in interest rates. Nonetheless, the world is now experiencing a heavy dose of *disinflation*. The economic consequences of that have almost always been nasty. A look at the history of the ebb and flow of some past inflations shows how much trouble we will experience.

CHAPTER 4

Analogies from Some Past

Inflations

There's nothing new about inflation. Chances are that it's been around since an early caveman found out that he didn't have enough meat and had to part with some of his most treasured goodies to get enough to feed his family. You can almost hear him complaining that saber-toothed tiger necklaces don't buy what they used to.

It's strange that nobody has found a clear and certain cure for this economic disease. What's more, since inflation always produces unpleasant results in the long run, you would think that some medicine to prevent it would have been developed long ago. But, when it first starts, it allows almost everyone to feel a sense of great prosperity, so that it is usually a very attractive short-term political expedience. Then, once it becomes strongly entrenched, the remedy is very painful. The necessity to inflict that pain is precisely Ronald Reagan's problem.

What is the cure? If you listen to what our politicians say, you get the idea that it's actually fairly cut and dried. But there hasn't been very much scientific evidence of a solution to the problem. Take the concept of cutting taxes that is getting such lip-service right now. Basically, the idea is to get the Government out of our hair by cutting Federal expenditures sharply, getting the budget into better balance, and counting on the tax cuts to provide the incentive to get production up to the point where there can be enough supply of goods to make prices level off. Cut taxes for both individuals and corporations, says the Roth–Kemp program. That sounds lovely to anyone who becomes sick and tired of seeing the amount that is deducted from his paycheck. Maybe it *will* work. Still, it's interesting to remember that only a few years ago almost everyone agreed that the way to lick inflation was to *raise* taxes, and certainly not to cut them. For example, President Johnson has been roundly criticized for not paying for the Vietnam War through tax increases rather than through heavier Federal debt. So let's not be carried away by the fact that cutting taxes could feel so good. In spite of all of the assurances of today's experts, no one really knows that it will work out without making necessary a great many additional measures that would cause a good deal of disruption in our economic system.

The basic formula for inflation is simple enough. It's that there is too much money chasing too few goods. That was relatively easy to detect in the good old days when money was represented by metallic coins. Whenever the people in power decided that it would be convenient to make the supply of money go further, they simply skimmed off some of the gold or silver from the coins, or used a baser metal. That pushed the supply of money higher and some sort of inflation became inevitable. Naturally, the process became more widespread when paper money replaced metal. It was much easier to print more paper than to shave the amount of metal in coins. Also, it was much more difficult to detect! If the paper money was backed by gold or some other form of valuable, the decrease in the amount of backing could be kept a deep dark secret until it was too late for the public to complain. But, even printing money was a simple process compared to the present, when the world's supply of money depends on credit and on the amount of debt that the Government allows to get on the books. By simply pumping up the amount of reserves that banks have on hand to allow them to lend money, the supply that reaches the economic system can be increased enormously, and inflation can creep up on us without giving anyone but the banking experts any advanced warning. Besides, just as the process of inflating grows more complicated, so does the kind of medicine that is required to cure it.

Basically, there are three factors that are involved in causing prices to skyrocket. The most typical is the creation of too much money and credit. Naturally, that means that most people who want to buy something can find the available money. That's the kind of thing that happens during wartime, when so huge a part of the country's production goes to the military that there really isn't much left over for the civilian population, even though it keeps earning just as much or more money. One way of controlling this has been through rationing or through price controls. It works during periods of patriotic fervor, but it just postpones the day of reckoning. Once peace has been declared, the accumulated demand and all the money which couldn't be spent pours out to buy in a market which still doesn't have the advantage of full production. Prices really begin to skyrocket. This kind of pressure produces what has come to be known as demand-pull inflation.

Still another trigger for rapidly rising prices comes from an upward push in the cost of production—the so-called cost-push variety of inflation. That can come about for a variety of reasons. Typically, labor demands more pay, and the extra expense isn't matched by an offsetting increase in productivity. Or raw material costs increase. We've seen an example of that in the last eight years when the cost of oil has skyrocketted. Energy is so fundamental to everything in the industrialized world that it has caused an upward push that has spread to a vast number of things. Since no one can expect manufacturers to operate at a loss for very long, it is quite anticipateable that they will attempt to pass along their additional cost of doing business to the ultimate buyer. This type of inflation is very persistent because it becomes circular. The more prices rise, the more labor want pay increases and the more producers want for their raw materials. The cure is almost always an abrupt and painful shock to the economic system.

Either of these two price pushers tend to be associated with a third and even more damaging effect—that of inflationary expectations. It's only natural that anyone living through a period of rapidly rising prices tends to think that anything he doesn't buy today will cost even more tomorrow. The other side of the coin is that anything that he sells would be worth more if he holds on to it. So there is a great deal of buying of things that might not be immediately needed, coupled with a tendency to withhold goods from the market. The result is to keep a number of things in relatively short supply and to cause rising prices to begin to accelerate as the velocity of the use of money increases. But, there's one good thing about inflationary expectations! Since to a large extent they are psychological, they can be changed with relatively less difficulty than either demand–pull or cost–push inflation. Curbing these expectations is the easiest way to make a dent in inflation. There are a number of ways to do that and they vary considerably according to the conditions at the time. The one thing that they have in common is the feeling that the political leaders will be tough enough to bite the bullet and to stay with their struggle for a prolonged period of time, if necessary. It is likely that there will be a major continuing effort by the Reagan Administration to convince us that it will do just that. Once the feeling that there's a possibility of a downturn in prices enters the awareness of the public, the tide can be turned.

Inflation at times can be a short-lived phenomenon, usually caused by an event without too much staying power. But the inflations that have been very troublesome have been long-lasting affairs. Take the inflation we are struggling with now. It became nastier until quite recently, and has, therefore, attracted more attention. But, prices have been rising more or less steadily since the beginning of World War II—and that's some 40 years ago. During those years, we've had some periods of stability, but for the most part, the course had been steadily upward, and almost all of the post-War Presidents have tried to do something about it. The trouble that they have had—and they've shared it with other leaders in history who have also had to face rising prices—is that periods of inflation are also periods of prosperity during which most people fare pretty well. While they complain continually as they pay more and more for what they want, they are also making more money and living better. As a result, the early years of a long inflationary spiral are usually welcome and it isn't until it has reached a later and more virulent stage that there is really a desire to do something about it. That's been true throughout history. The problem is that the solution is usually to end the prosperity and, for a while, that feels much worse than even a rapidly escalating inflation. So most political leaders try to avoid actually committing themselves to the ending of inflation even though they often speak quite strongly against it. They've kept from acting until it was forced upon them.

Since there is a considerable history of inflation, we may be able to get some ideas of just what to do by taking a backward glance at some of the important price crises of the past.

Case History 1: Lions for the Christians, Price Controls for the Masses

When Diocletian became Emperor of Rome in 284 A.D., he had a clear mandate to change the way in which things were being run. Not that he had been elected by the public! That wasn't how it was done in ancient Rome. Like many previous rulers, he was brought into power by the army. But he had inherited quite a mess to clean up. By the end of the third century, the glory that was Rome had become tarnished. Diocletian, who seemed to be a thoughtful type even though he had grown up in army camps, looked exactly like the kind of person to reverse the downward course. Above all, he had the advantage of being politically conservative, which was very attractive to the military rulers who had begun to long for a return to the good old days.

As he came to power he was confronted with a weakened military position along many of the far-flung frontiers of the Empire, where so-called barbarians were in open revolt. As if that weren't enough, the economic structure of Rome was shaken by inflation. The Emperors who had preceded him were military men with little or no interest in civilian affairs. When they needed money, they simply taxed the population to the breaking point. When that didn't provide enough money, they began to debase the currency that had once made Rome such a powerful economic force. The very basis of the trade that the Empire was able to carry out within the vast regions it controlled was the fact that every one could count on the gold solidi, and on the denarius, which had been largely silver. Those coins were a common denominator in all of the diverse regions and cultures under Roman control. But by the time Diocletian took over, the amount of gold in the solidi had been diminished, and the denarius wasn't even good copper. Some of the Emperors had decided to plate it with tin, while pretending that it had the same value as the old coin. The Romans didn't have the advantage of knowing Gresham's law, but it operated nonetheless. The good money that was left was hoarded and the worthless tin-plated coins took over. Naturally, the price of commodities started to rise. That was pleasant enough for the rich landowners, but it made trade within the Empire very difficult and the populations of the outlying regions became more restless than ever. There were a seemingly endless series of rebellions to crush. Perhaps the most threatening effect of all was that the army was increasingly unhappy because it could no longer count on the purchasing power of its pay. The Roman Empire looked as though it was about to fall apart.

Diocletian mounted an attack on these problems with a combination of an unorthodox set of actions on the military front and a return to strict orthodoxy on the home front. Strangely enough, that's much the same sort of combination that is being proposed by the Reagan Administration. For the military, Diocletian chose a completely new approach. He divided the Empire into four parts and appointed a plenipotentiary Caesar with authority rivaling his own as the Governor of each of the sectors. The results were excellent. With decentralization, each military Caesar was able to understand the local problems far better than a single Emperor had been. As a result, Rome was finally able to contain the belligerent populations of the frontiers.

With that success accomplished, the Emperor proceeded to reinstate the glory of the old-time monarchs. He considered himself a God, and demanded the pomp and circumstances that had been ignored by the rough and tumble military men who had occupied the throne before him. It had some terrible effects. The return to a more rigid observance of the orthodox religion led to a new look at the Christian minority which had been relatively unmolested for a number of years. Since Diocletian couldn't tolerate a competing religion, the situation of the Christians grew worse and worse. By the end of Diocletian's reign, they suffered the worst persecution that had ever been seen. It wasn't to last for very long, and perhaps the very violence of the attacks wore out the prejudice against them. In any event, within 20 years Constantine the Great had become Emperor and had installed the Christian religion as the most powerful force of Rome. But, while the persecutions lasted, they were bloody, and they tarnished Diocletian's name in history in spite of his clear ability as an administrator and the temporary preserver of the power of Rome.

On a more constructive level, Diocletian's new conservative approach called for a return to a reliable monetary system. His first step was to reinstate the gold content of the solidi. A few years later, he did the same for the silver coin. Finally, he made the denarius a copper coin, but one that was considerably better than the tin-plated affair that had become virtually worthless. Actually, the copper coin became the most widely circulated of all, since the gold and silver coins were the most convenient form for the Government to insist on when it collected taxes from merchants and money lenders. Since the new copper money had some real value, it worked out fairly well. Except, that is, for the army and the tax collectors. Since they weren't quite satisfied with the purchasing power of the denarius, Diocletian followed the example of some of his predecessors and had his tax collectors assess landowners and merchants a certain amount of their production and collected in merchandise or produce rather than money. It put a premium on the ability of the tax collectors and, of course, it also encouraged graft. The result was a rapid increase in the ranks of the Civil Service; and a rise in the cost of Government. Perhaps it prophesied the state of affairs of the middle of the twentieth century—almost 1700 years later. Even then, the necessity to allow the tax collector to examine one's business and to decide how much one should pay made them about as popular as the IRS is in the United States today. The middle class complained that it was being obliterated, and the peasants felt as though they were being reduced to serfdom.

While reinstating the real value of money did some good, inflation was too well entrenched to give way easily. So, in 301 A.D. Diocletian imposed price controls along with an Imperial Proclamation that appealed for patriotism. It's the first detailed account we have of the fixing of prices, although we know that there were other such attempts in the ancient world.

To get an idea of why prices had skyrocketted enough to force the wage–price edict, just look at what happened to the silver content of the widely circulated denarius from the time of Nero:

Silver Content of Roman Coin of Denomination

Issuing Authority	Percent Silver
Nero 54 A.D.	94
Vitellius 68 A.D.	81
Domitian 81 A.D.	92
Trajan 98 A.D.	93
Hadrian 117 A.D.	87
Antoninus Pius 138 A.D.	75
Marcus Aurelius 161 A.D.	68
Septimius Severus 193 A.D.	50
Elagabalus 218 A.D.	43
Alexander Severus 222 A.D.	35
Gordian 238 A.D.	28
Philip 244 A.D.	0.5
Claudius Victorinus 268 A.D.	0.02

The Diocletian control measure is particularly interesting because it gives an idea of how complex an economy there was in Rome before its fall. There's not much doubt that inflation had a large share in bringing about the eventual collapse, although it took a long time to come. Still, at Diocletian's time, there were a surprisingly large number of items that seemed necessary to control. What's more, the list isn't complete, because freight rates from various parts of the Empire were also price-fixed:

Number of Prices and Wages Covered by Edict

Prices

Foods	222
Hides and leather	87
Timber and wood products	94
Textiles and clothing	385
Wicker and grass products	32
Cosmetics, ointments, incense	53
Precious metals	17
Miscellaneous	31

Wages

General, skilled, and unskilled	76
Silk workers and embroiderers	13
Wool weavers	6
Fullers	26

There were teeth in this law, unlike some of it's equivalents in the twentieth century, where violators all too often wind up with nothing much more than a slap on the wrist. Diocletian's penalty for violating the price control law was death. But in spite of that, the law was almost impossible to enforce, and finally gave way to the difficulties of communication throughout the Empire. So prices continued to rise. Gold, in terms of the copper denarius, soared by 250% during the period of controls, and prices of other commodities continued to increase. Four years after his price control order, Diocletian resigned as Emperor, citing the usual reasons of poor health. Perhaps it was out of frustration over the fact that his attempt had not worked out better, but, actually, his program did do the job. It stabilized prices just enough to slow down the run-away increases and it allowed order to be re-established within the Empire. Not only did it stop the tide which was threatening to engulf Rome, but it allowed time to get the frontiers under reasonable control. It made it possible for Constantine to take office in 324 A.D. and to have enough to work with so that he could earn the title of "The Great."

The improvement might have lasted even longer than Constantine's 13-year reign. But the Emperors who succeeded him just couldn't resist the temptation to devalue the currency once again. By the end of the century, Egyptian wheat had gone up 100-fold, and the price of gold was up 5000%. Julian the Apostate tried price controls once again 60 years after the Diocletian attempt, but it was too late. The post-Diocletian inflation had so sapped the strength of the Empire that there was nothing left to do but to move it to Constantinople and to start all over again.

The Analogy for Our Time

You can huff and puff until you blow your house down, but there's no way in which you can beat demand–pull inflation until you put your monetary system on a solid footing. Price controls can buy some time, but they can't do the job unless there is a patriotic fervor to support them. Even at that, they can't be kept in force for any prolonged period of time without running into a horde of violators. Even today, when we have far better communications than the Roman Empire, there is no way to enforce controls without filling all of the jails to capacity. A combination that has at least some chance of working is to get the monetary system on a sound basis and to *keep* it that way, while using price controls to stall until enough goods can be pushed into the market to satisfy demand. That technique worked out in Germany after World War II. The country was being run by the Army of Occupation, which had as much power as any emperor, and no particular desire to become popular. At the very beginning of the post-war period, the new Administrators pumped a large amount of money into the system and established wage and price controls. One of the results was a black market which became quite notorious. It absorbed a good deal of the excess money supply, even though it accounted for only about 10% of all transactions. But the Army of Occupation had no need to capitulate. It stuck to its guns. Above all, it kept the money supply under strict control after the first injection. Naturally, prices had a large one-time jump when controls were lifted. But that had been pretty well anticipated and, with money staying tight, it was the last major upward push of prices for a long time. For the most part, after the jump was over and the monetary system had been reformed, industrious West Germans were able to go to work and to build their economy until it was the strongest on the Continent.

There was a similar effort in the United States during the Nixon Administration. In 1969, the supply of credit was tightened and within a couple of years a variety of wage and price control measures were put into effect. Unfortunately for the control program, the Federal Reserve didn't have the staying power. It allowed the money supply to grow and interest rates to tumble. Naturally, that caused a period of rejoicing for the financial markets, but it allowed inflation to begin all over again. Even before President Ford took over from Nixon, inflation had become the main problem.

So the lesson of the Diocletian price control experiment is clear enough. Stop debasing your money. If you do, other measures have a chance of succeeding. If not, almost anything you do to combat inflation is doomed to failure. Since it's credit that accounts for most of today's money supply, it is up to the Fed to keep it growing at a very slow pace. It's very difficult for most political leaders to stick with the resultant high interest rates and business problems that result. We'll see whether Ronald Reagan and Chairman Volker can do it!

Case History 2: Saved From the Plague, but not From Wage Controls

Late in 1347, the Bubonic Plague hit Europe with all of the force of an atomic bomb attack or, more appropriately, with the effect of one of those neutron bombs which destroy the population while leaving property intact. It all began in October 1347 when a Genovese galley with dead or dying men at the oars put into a port in Sicily. Within three years the plague they carried had wiped out about one-third of the population of Europe. Perhaps the most frightening part was that medicine was in such a primitive state that no one knew just what was happening or where it would hit next.

Bubonic Plague is a disease that originates in rats and also in the tiny fleas which infest them. With sanitary conditions the way they were in the Middle Ages, rats were a constant home companion, to which no one paid very much attention. Of course, it would have been incredible to the medieval mind to believe that there were such insignificant carriers of so gigantic a calamity. In fact, it wasn't until some 500 years later that the cause of the disease was finally established. So the medieval philosophers were free to create all kinds of explanations. Perhaps, it was a concoction of the devil, or perhaps retribution by God for the multiple sins of mankind. Some astrologers were convinced that the planets had caused polluted air and were responsible for what grew to be known as the Black Death. They pointed out that the skies had given a highly unusual signal back in March 1345, when no less than three planets were in the Constellation of Aquarius—Saturn, Jupiter, and Mars. Others, more earth-bound, tried some of the more typical remedies. There were always the traditional scapegoats, the Jews. They were accused of poisoning the wells and were persecuted savagely until it began to occur to many people that the Jews were dying of the Black Death just like everyone else. But no matter what cure was attempted, nothing seemed to work. The plague was strangely democratic for its time. It hit the rich and the poor alike, although it was at its worst in the crowded slums of the cities.

The disease made itself even more confusing by taking three different forms. The first and simplest to see was characterized by the appearance of buboes, or swellings in the groin or armpits. It was possible to recover from this form of the disease. The second, and more deadly, variety was characterized by the spitting of blood and by violent pains in the chest. It was the pneumonic version and was terribly contagious. The third developed in the blood stream and killed within a very short period of time—often in no more than a few hours. Since a man could go to bed healthy and wake up dead, this form of the plague encouraged the belief that either God or the Devil was at work.

The amount of havoc that was wrought in the first year made Hiroshima look like a day in the country. In some areas the death count was as high as 70% of the population. Florence lost something more than 60% of its inhabitants. Then, within a few years, it was over, although there were recurrences from time to time. However, it left the world terribly shaken. The effects on the moral and social life of the fourteenth century were not, perhaps, as profound as the loss of life. Nonetheless, there were some important changes.

During the Middle Ages, every factor of life was well-structured, and most people accepted their role, even though it could very well be an unpleasant one. But after the plague, a number of the most respected institutions came under challenge. The Church, which had been important, didn't escape. Some of the more devout formed into bands of penitents, and became flagellants who beat themselves publicly while begging for God's mercy. As the plague took its toll, these groups grew in importance. They called on the officials of the Church to give up their extravagances and to return to the simpler way of Jesus. Sexual morals degenerated as well. The taboos against sex seemed much less important, since the Black Death would kill you whether you were virtuous or not. In addition, there was suddenly an appearance of a great many heirs for property. Since, in a number of cases entire families had been wiped out, it was often necessary to look for very distant relatives to find the next-of-kin. Also, the onslaught of the plague was so swift and unexpected that a great many people of property died intestate. One of the results of the great switch in property ownership was a rapid increase in the number of fortune hunters, who would try to charm the newly rich heirs into marriage. Another was that family fortunes that had been quite well-handled because the money had been around for generations suddenly fell into the hands of people who were quite frankly *nouveau riche*. Their behavior in some cases became outrageous, which caused a considerable amount of tongue-clucking by the neighbors, and especially by those members of the clergy who were still alive.

But the upheaval in the morality of the post-plague societies was of minor importance compared to what happened to the labor force. After all, the Middle Ages functioned on manpower, and with large percentages of the population wiped out, there just weren't enough workers to be had. So, after a brief pause to let the shock of the Black Death wear off, workingmen began to demand more and more. Not that there were any unions as yet! But it wasn't hard for a depleted work-force to demand more money. That happened in some of the textile factories of France. But, the largest and longest-lasting effect was felt in England.

England was particularly hard hit by the Black Death. Approximately half the population was wiped out. It was a particularly devastating blow for the country that had been so successful in beating the flower of French knighthood. But the destruction was so great that large farms were literally deserted, and big landowners could no longer sustain their operation of their huge estates. Since wealth in the fourteenth century, especially for the nobility, was a function of land ownership and how many people there were to work it (and also to keep the nobleman and his family comfortable), the loss of household servants as well as peasants caused a great change in the well-being of the rich. In fact, so many people were deserting the back-breaking work of the fields and looking for cushy jobs in the towns at much higher pay, that relative values of land and labor were simply reversed. Rents declined as an inducement to keep them down on the farm. Even with that, a great deal of land was allowed to return to wilderness. In the cities and at manufacturing facilities workers were demanding and getting 2 to 3 times the pre-plague salaries.

Naturally, inflation began to push prices up. It was an

untypical inflation. There was plenty of property around, and it was worth less than it had been previously. Great houses and estates were being sold at a very low price. But, the price of food was on the rise, as was that for any service that was needed. Currency was sound and there was enough to account for some upward push in prices, since there were less goods available than before the plague struck. But this was really a *cost-push* inflation since the extra expense of labor could not possibly be offset by an increase in productivity. Faced with a difficult economic situation and one which was unfavorable for his nobles, what could have been more natural for Edward III than to impose wage controls! In 1349, he issued an ordinance rolling back pay to the 1347 level. That didn't work out very well, so in 1351, with the blessings of Parliament, the Statute of Laborers was issued. It not only set wage controls, but denounced the idle and the beggars, and established some severe penalties.

Anyone in the twentieth century would have been able to tell Edward III that wage controls won't work. Unfortunately, he didn't know that. The prisons began to be filled with violators, and eventually the problems intensified from outspoken discontent to outright revolt. In 1381 more money was needed by the monarchy to carry on its conquest of France. So, it imposed a poll tax. Ordinarily, taxpayers would have simply grumbled a bit, but they would have paid up. But after 20 years of being diddled out of what people thought was their rightful pay increases, they were in no mood for it. Some 60 thousand rebels, led by Wat Tyler and John Ball, poured into London. Richard II, then a mere 14-year-old lad, took refuge in the Tower of London. But then he decided to come out and meet with the rebels. He convinced them that he was their King too and agreed to reasonable rents and freedom in negotiating wages. The rebels fell for it, but they were soon to be sorry. Wat Tyler was killed in a scuffle with the Mayor of London and King Richard not only went back on all of his promises, but he even rounded up and executed thousands of the rebels. Perhaps it accounts for the relative ease with which Bolingbroke was able to seize the crown a few years later. In the subsequent mix-up of rebellion and further victories in France, the cost–push inflation eventually cooled down and reached stability. But it took years.

The Analogy for Our Time

It takes a great deal instability to get a cost–push inflation going, much more than to start a boiling demand–pull type by something as simple as debasing the currency. But, once a cost–push really starts, especially if it involves labor, it is terribly difficult to stop. Ask President Carter, who tried his best to get his friends in the labor movement to accept wage guidelines, only to have to keep pretending that they were being lived up to when, in reality, they were falling apart. Or, better still, ask the Soviet Union, which must decide whether to put down labor movements all around its Empire, since the demands for more pay and shorter hours keep arising. The Soviet stilled them in Czechoslovakia in the 1960s, but it will be difficult for it to put down the aftermaths of Polish union activity. If so, it will have to decide how to end the inflation which has started the entire movement on its way.

To cure cost–push inflation without force is something that requires some fairly creative thinking. How, for example, can we get OPEC to keep from imposing price increases as soon as they possibly can? Or how can we ask the labor unions to tolerate the erosion in paychecks without demanding that it be made up by wage increases? There are two ways to go; one is a short-term method, which is extremely unpleasant. The other is long-term, and is very nice indeed. Perhaps that's why we have been hearing so much about the long-term method and so little about the short. Long term, the way to end cost–push is to increase productivity. That can be done by building new, more efficient plants and by either developing better ways to use energy or developing new sources. The Reagan idea is that it can be accomplished by kind words, less regulation, and tax incentives.

There's no reason to doubt it, but how long will it take?

Most business executives aren't likely to be in any hurry to build new facilities just to gain a tax benefit until they can be sure that the economy will be good enough to take the product they will be producing. So, it is likely to be slow going at first. The new supply-side economics is promising enough and it certainly holds out hope of starting us out on a better direction. But, it will be quite a while until the increased efficiency that it promotes becomes widespread enough to pull prices down!

Then there's the short-term way. It can stop cost-push more rapidly, but no one wants to be the first to use it. It's to allow a recession to develop, and then to *let it continue for a long enough time so that it gets painful and scary*. Without the determination to stick with it, it's a waste of time and resources. For example, the possibility of a run-away inflation because of Afghanistan and Iran early in 1980 so worried the Federal Reserve and President Carter that they were willing to push to economy into recession. It began as a fast, deep one. Too deep, in fact. Because it frightened them into relenting, the recession became the shortest on record. At first OPEC was a little discouraged, and the Saudis talked of stabilized oil prices. Labor was equally worried, but once again the downturn didn't last for long enough to cause them to level off their demands. In fact, even while production was sliding at a precipitous rate in the Spring of 1980, wages were increasing sharply.

We have enough historical evidence to show us what must be done if we are going to end the cost-push with any reasonable period of time. We have a recent example of a number of unions which are very sensibly willing to make concessions rather than face the loss of jobs. The answer is that we must accept a business downturn and live with it until it becomes frightening enough to threaten massive unemployment and a far smaller demand for oil and other commodities. The Carter Administration prevented anything such as that from developing, so no wonder we have encouraged the cost-push! The question confronting the United States right now is this: President Reagan did not have to do much to allow a recession to begin. All he needs to do now is to avoid any dramatic actions to prevent it from deepening. Will he have the courage to sit it out until it has a chance to be effective?

Case History 3: Don't Strike it Too Rich

When Columbus discovered America, he brought home a number of curious things which pleased his sponsor, Queen Isabella. But, it made very little difference to the economies of Europe. The big change came 30 or 40 years later as a result of the efforts of the Conquistadors. In 1519, Cortez sailed from Cuba with only about 400 Spaniards, and within two years he had taken Mexico City. Then, 10 years later, Pizarro landed in Peru with less than 200 men and in less than two years, he had defeated an army of 40,000 Incas and captured their King and horde of his nobles. Such feats were not only the dream stuff of their own time, but also of Hollywood movies over 400 years later. The immediate economic effect came from a huge plunder of gold and silver. Cortez took the treasures of the Aztecs and sent them back to Spain. Even that wasn't as great as Pizarro's loot. After he captured the Inca King, he offered to release him and his nobles for a ransom of enough gold to fill a room 22 feet long 17 feet wide, and 9 feet high. The Incas paid the ransom, but Pizarro broke his word and put his captives to death. In addition to marking a black day for the Spanish, it might have been a costly mistake. The Indians in other parts of the Inca Empire had some large stockpiles of treasure. But when the news reached them of Pizarro's betrayal, they took out their gold and buried it. They did a pretty good job of hiding because, in spite of countless searches, no sign of the buried treasure has appeared.

In any event, by the 1530s, the amount of gold imported into Spain began to increase sharply. It reached its peak during the ten years from 1551-1560, when it was almost 10 times the amount received 20 years earlier. At that time, there was undoubtedly a large amount of illegal importation and outright smuggling that would swell that total still higher. But, even that astonishing increase of the amount of the yellow metal was vastly exceeded by the increase in the amount of silver. In 1545, a huge silver mine was opened in Potesi, Peru. The little mining town greatly expanded into a rollicking, violent, drunken city of 120,000, making it easily the largest city in the Americas. At just about the same time, several huge mines were also devel-oped in Mexico. The Indians were exploited as very low cost labor, and the treasure ships of Spain were kept very busy bringing silver back to the old country. The peak of the shipments wasn't reached until about 1600, and by then it was running at almost 200 times the amount of the 1520s. Examine the best estimates of the amounts that arrived in Spain over a prolonged period of time, as calculated and researched by the brilliant economist, Earl Hamilton.

Total Decennial Imports of Fine Gold and Silver
(in grams)

Period	Silver	Gold
1503–1510	—	4,965,180
1511–1520	—	9,153,220
1521–1530	148,739	4,889,050
1531–1540	86,193,876	14,466,360
1541–1550	177,573,164	24,957,130
1551–1560	303,121,174	42,620,080
1561–1570	942,858,792	11,530,940
1571–1580	1,118,591,954	9,429,140
1581–1590	2,103,027,689	12,101,650
1591–1600	2,707,626,528	19,451,420
1601–1610	2,213,631,245	11,764,090
1611–1620	2,192,255,993.	8,855,940
1621–1630	2,145,339,043	3,889,760
1631–1640	1,396,759,594	1,240,400
1641–1650	1,056,430,966	1,549,390
1651–1660	443,256,546	469,430
Totals 1503–1660	16,886,815,303	181,333,180

This influx of precious metals was something like hitting the biggest jackpot of all times. Spain became rich and its new-found wealth soon spread out throughout all of Europe. The amount of coins made of precious metals that jangled in the pockets of Europeans by the middle of the seventeenth century had grown to 3-4 times that which had been circulating at the beginning of the sixteenth century. Of course, there was no way in which the amount of new money could be matched by an equivalent increase in the amount of goods being produced. You can guess the rest. The result was a prolonged inflation which became known to historians as the "Price Revolution."

The inflation started in the region of Cadiz and Seville near the ports through which Spain received the principal shipments of American treasure. It then spread rapidly throughout Spain and then to Italy and France and finally to the countries of Northern Europe. In a little over 60 years from the time that the huge shipments of American gold and silver began, the prices of goods in Spain had tripled. Labor, of course, was slow in catching up with the advance, although by the first decade of the seventeenth century, helped by a new plague that killed off many laborers, Spanish workers finally were able to match the rise in prices. But, for many years the great bonanza of the Americas was hardly a pleasure for them. Before the sixteenth century was completed, even the King of Spain, troubled by constant reversals in war and the need to hold together an Empire that had grown too stretched out, finally decided to make ends meet by debasing the coinage, of all things! So much for striking it rich! Inflation killed off the benefits in a surprisingly short time.

However, the influx of gold and silver and the subsequent "price revolution" *did* change the way of the world. In fact, even before the Spanish conquest, Henry the Navigator, Prince of Portugal, began to develop larger ships and used them to explore the African coast and to eventually carve out new routes to the East. By breaking the monopoly that Venice had held for centuries over the spice and dye trade, the Portuguese initiated a switch from the cities that had formerly dominated the commerce of the Middle Ages to some booming cities on the Atlantic Coast. That switch was also helped by increasing amounts of silver from newly discovered mines in Austria. Of course, it was nothing compared with the influx from the New World, but it helped allow a new group of merchants and money lenders and bankers to function with money that could be respected across international borders. The result was the multiplying of international commerce, spurred by an increasingly large and prosperous middle class. When the precious metals from Spain also hit the market, and produced inflation, the old-time landowners began to suffer. They counted on rents and refused to engage in commerce. Soon, unless they were extremely rich, they began to run out of money. The growing middle class was able to buy large chunks of land from them, thus beginning the bridging of the abyss which had existed between the nobility and the middle classes. It was a process that was to create new aggregations of wealth powerful enough to break down the old order. How strange it would have seemed to an observer who contemplated the future in the early part of the sixteenth century! Who would have believed that hitting the jackpot would result in the impoverishment of its winner—Spain? Only centuries later would economists understand that having too much money can be just as bad for a country as having too little.

The Analogy for Our Time

It isn't often that history has given us an example of the kind of bonanza that Spain experienced in the mid-sixteenth century. Interestingly enough, we have had one of those rare happenings right in our own generation. It is, of course, OPEC, and the explosion in oil prices that it has engineered. Actually, in terms of money, it probably dwarfs the Spanish experience. There are some significant differences, however. For one thing, when the Spanish plundered the Indian treasure, it did not interfere with the economies of the European world, except to propel them first to greater prosperity and then to inflation. OPEC, on the other hand, has drained the industrialized world of countless billions. In fact, it started an inflationary process immediately by increasing the cost of everything that uses energy and that, of course, spread out into many items that aren't usually considered particularly energy-dependent, as labor unions demanded more pay to keep up with the extra expenses the workingman was facing. Even welfare programs cost more, and the expense of medicine and hospitilization increased dramatically. In effect, the OPEC price increases made it difficult for the Western world to continue to meet its social programs *and* to pay for crude oil. Not being willing to give up either one, the industrialized countries had no choice but to go heavily into hock and to increase their national debts to close to the danger point—at least to the point where it became impossible to avoid inflation.

Of course, inflation hit the OPEC countries right away. They had little productive capacity of their own, and many of them have very large and very poor populations. The things that they had to buy from abroad, and the higher prices of the industrialized countries, were imposed on the oil producers. The extra money that was floating around in those formerly marginal countries merely amplified the inflation. But, some of the countries were unique, particularly Saudi Arabia, the Arab Emirates, and a few of the other nations on the Arabian Gulf. They were different than most of the other members of OPEC in that their populations were very small, and their Governments strong and authoritative. Their technique was not the same as the others. Saudi Arabia is particularly interesting because its cash receipts are so high. It could not avoid inflation, but its rulers had learned a lesson from past history. It was impossible to avoid a large increase in consumption, and that meant importing a great many things from the industrialized countries. But, the lion's share of the Saudi great wealth is being used for the building great productive facilities. If the oil ever runs out, or a substitute is found, Saudi Arabia intends to have very large means of producing other things. That involves importing not only skilled technicians, but also ordinary workers. Since that imposes a political risk for the sheltered Saudis, it is nice for the rulers that they be clearly identifiable as foreigners. For example, a great many of the laborers in the country are imported from Korea.

Even with as large a capital investment plan as the traffic will bear, Saudi Arabia still has a tremendous amount of excess cash. Partly in order to keep it from hitting the consumer spending circuit, which could only cause an acceleration of inflation, and partly to keep the consumers of oil from running out of liquidity, the Saudi Government has become the world's biggest lender. It has bought huge amounts of Treasuries in the United States and of the Government bonds of other countries as well. But even that doesn't dent their resources. So, the banking system of the international community has been called upon to "recycle" the Saudi petrodollars (payment for petroleum is still in dollars, in spite of all of the complaints by some of the Arab extremists). That is, the banks take in the deposits of the Saudis and lend the money to other countries. The most desireable of such loans from the Arab point of view is to the underdeveloped countries. But, of course, that means some pretty fancy risk-taking for the banks who lend to some of the African or South American countries.

There's no question Saudi Arabia has learned from Spain and has added some new notions of her own. But, it's not all a bed of roses for us. Any change in the Saudi leadership or in her attitude toward the United States could produce a major explosion in the world's financial health. After all, if the banker of the world decides to become unpleasant, it can make us all a great deal poorer.

What's more, while it's clear that the Saudi leaders have learned well, it isn't nearly so obvious about the rest of us. Will we continue to dance to OPEC's tune? Or will we decide that a tougher approach is in order? Most importantly, will we spend the amount of time and effort that is required to develop new energy resources. So far, our record has been dismal. If it continues to be, we are no better than a hostage to adventurous politicians in countries that export oil.

Case History 4: Man the Printing Presses

Even before the hyperinflation in Germany during 1923 had begun, one bewildered observer remarked that he had to pay the huge sum of 5000 marks for a cup of coffee. But, he said, before he had gotten through drinking it, the price had gone up to 8000 marks. Later on in the year, people made sure that they did their marketing in the morning, since if they waited until evening their purchasing power could well have been halved. It wasn't uncommon to see housewives pushing wheelbarrows full of marks when they went shopping for their groceries. Germany, in 1923, went through what was undoubtedly the craziest inflation of all times. Perhaps that is why the alarmists who warn us about the impending doom that threatens the United States keep referring to that period as though it can happen here at any moment. But the situations are so dissimiliar that the probability of anything like the German inflation striking us is about as low as that of the Earth colliding with the Moon. So, a look at just what happened in post-World War I Germany should be somewhat comforting.

At the end of the war, Germany had lost 13% of its territory, about 40% of its national wealth, and its industrial production declined to 42% of the pre-war level. Much of Europe was in a similar situation. France was almost as badly off, and England's wartime losses were severe. Early in 1919, soon after the armistice, the amount of paper money in circulation in Germany was about six times that of 1913. Since production was only 42% of the pre-war days, the increase in paper marks meant that the currency–production ratio had increased by about 14-to-1. That was serious, but far from a forerunner to the terrible inflation that was to follow in a few years. As a matter of fact, partly because higher prices stimulated production and partly because of the determination of the German people to recover from the war, the economy really began to improve.

German Industrial Production
(Last prewar year = 100)

Post-War I years	Weimar Republic area 1913 = 100
1919	42
1920	61
1921	73
1922	80
1923	52
1924	78
1925	92
1926	89
1927	111
1928	114

By 1922, production was back to 80% of the pre-war level. Not a bad accomplishment in only four years! It was then that the victors of the war began to turn the screws. France and England were anxious to be repaid for the damages they had suffered during the war and a desire for revenge clouded their better judgment. Woodrow Wilson's problems at home kept the United States from exercising restraint. So, in May 1921, the Reparations Commission fixed a bill for the Germans to pay which was enough to break the back of any country, let alone one that had just been through an annihilating war. The amount to be paid held out little hope for relief, since it extended over a 30-year period. Germany was to fork over not only a huge amount of cash, but also about 26% of the proceeds of her exports, among other things. Until that point, the German budget nearly had been brought into balance, and the value of the mark was relatively stable in the international markets. But the Reparations demands ended all of that. The mark was lowered to about one-third of its value and, as a consequence, wholesale prices tripled. That began the circular effect that was to produce the worst inflation on record before it ran its course. As the expenses of paying off the victors in the war grew, so did the expenses of Government.

The choice before the weak leaders of Germany was either to raise taxes or to print money. Raising taxes was slow and difficult, so naturally the decision was to print more money. After that, the downslide in the value of the mark began in earnest, until by mid-1923 things that had once cost one mark were literally selling for billions. The final blow came when France and Belgium occupied the industrial Ruhr valley as punishment for German defaults on their payments. That caused the local political leaders to organize a passive resistance, and it was all the Government needed. It simply abandoned all restraint and printed new money just as fast as the presses could handle it.

The end of the inflation came with an abrupt suddenness. In October 1923 a newly established Central Bank issued new paper currency, which had a base of land holdings, building and some business enterprises. Each of these new Rentenmarks was exchanged for 1 trillion old marks. Such was the desire of the German people for some sort of stability that they accepted the new money as though they could put their hands on the underlying assets, although such a course of action would have presented very difficult problems. The exchange worked! The new currency not only ended the inflation, but it also allowed the German economy to resume its upward march until by 1928, industrial production was at 114% of the pre-war level. In fact, it took the worldwide depression of the 1930s to end the German expansion, and then deflation succeeded inflation as the main villain.

The inflation had made life difficult for the poor, but it made it easy for those who had producing assets or who were clever enough to manipulate with foreign exchange to become much richer. Unfortunately, the middle class was eliminated, and those frugal citizens who had squirreled away savings were left with nothing at all. Just as an example of how badly fixed debt worked out, the entire mortgage debt outstanding before the war could have been paid off in 1923 for less than it cost to buy a glass of beer. The bitterness which resulted paved the way for the rise of Hitler. So, the German inflation was horrible, and the after-effects were even more horrible. But it did one good thing! It scared all of the industrial powers right up until the present time. Every time any European country begins to see its inflation rate rise rapidly, its leaders think of 1923 in Germany and shudder.

The Analogy for Our Time

The German inflation is in no way comparable to anything that is likely to happen in the United States. So, it's easy to ignore all of those raven-like croakings from the prophets of doom and despair who are doing us all a disservice by worrying about artificial problems and distracting us from trying to do something about the very real problems. The German inflation needed a combination of a weakening of production because of the war, a Government which couldn't fight its way out of a paper bag, and a couple of neighbors who were so angry that they wanted to strip Germany to the bone. All of that has no resemblance at all to a strong United States which is operating its plants below capacity and keeps trying to fight inflation rather than causing it to accelerate.

In any event, the risk in our country doesn't come from the printing presses nearly as much as from the over-extension of credit. In 1980 the amount of currency rose by about 12%. But the build-up of the money supply mostly represented by bank credit has been the main concern of our inflation watching. There's no question that it's growth has been one of the reasons for the inflation rate that we are now experiencing. Still, to approach the way in which the Germans handled themselves, the Federal Reserve would have to allow the money supply to double and then to double again several times after that. It's just as obvious as it can be that the Fed has no intention of allowing that to happen and that it is in a position to exercise control over its growth.

It's clear from the results of the German inflation that stabilizing the supply of money works out well. It may cause some economic difficulties and hit some sectors of the economy harder than others. But once the period of recession is over, Government policy can be free to turn from its continual attempt to dampen business in order to control inflation; it can begin to concentrate on aiding its growth instead. That might bring us to something more like the expansion of the 1960s than the depressing times of the 1970s. All that is needed is the courage on the part of the Federal Reserve Board and the Administration to keep a tight rein on the money supply until the recession gets deep enough to need help. That should allow disinflation to continue the course it has already begun. Throughout history, such times have been difficult for the economy as a whole, but they are made to order for those with cash to invest.

CHAPTER 5

And Now—Disinflation!

As one cynic pointed out, "The one thing we learn from history is that we *do* not learn from history." Not that those who are responsible for Government policy don't know about the past! It's just that they always seem quite sure that they can avoid the pitfalls and traps into which others fell. Perhaps it's that undeserved feeling of confidence that makes history have to repeat itself so often—and so dismally.

One of the easiest ways to lose confidence in the wisdom of policymakers is to watch them fighting battles that are already over, with just as much excitement and enthusiasm as if they were beginning, instead of ending. Take the way in which the Reagan Administration boasts about the fact that it is bringing inflation down. Of course it is! The battle against inflation is over; it's already been won. The new problem is that we have slipped into a disinflation that will last for some time and produce some nasty economic pain. But, no one in officialdom is saying anything about that. They are too busy boasting about their victory and planning ways in which to continue to attack the already defeated enemy.

Just look at some of the figures, if you want to get an idea of just how useless it is to keep on with the fight against inflation. During what was known as the "Great Price Depression" of the last part of the 19th Century, W. Layton, in his *Introduction to the History of Prices*, calculated that in the 25 or so years between the early 1870s and the late 1890s, 14 primary products, including basic minerals and textile raw materials, suffered a price slump of 35–43%. By comparison, a recent index of commodities showed a decline of 26% from the 1980 peak. Gold is down 60% and silver over 80%. Let's make some comparisons between the declines of some commodities then, and those during just the last two years here in the United States:

	Declines in the late 1890s	Declines in 1980 Recent Highs to Lows
Sugar	58%	43%
Petroleum	58%	25%
Cotton	54%	35%
Wheat	51%	34%
Wool	50%	14%
Pig-Iron	48%	Scrap steel 24%

It's not difficult to see that we have entered into a period that is more likely to be known for its price slump than for inflation. It's true that prices at the consumer level are slow to give ground. That's partly because of continued inflationary expectations and partly because of the way in which Government figures are kept. Any smart consumer knows that by shopping around a little, he can get large discounts from the retail price on almost any item that he wants. If price-cutting were taken into consideration, and added to the discounts available in housing prices by the use of seller-based financing, it would be clear that the period of price decline has already begun.

Feeding Inflation

Inflation is like a hungry tiger cub. Early in its life, it can't keep growing unless it is fed continually. Later, when it is full grown, it can survive for a while on its own fat—in this case on inflationary expectations. But even those expectations need feeding after a while, or the inflationary tiger will slim down and die. The best known food for inflation is war, and the United States had two of them in the same decade. That was enough to push prices to a high plateau. Even at that, our productive capacity was so great that President Eisenhower was able to contain the forward momentum with relatively mild measures. It was only after the Vietnam War and the Arab Oil Embargo that we found ourselves with a full-grown tiger, able to survive on expectations.

It's very popular now to blame inflation on the money supply and to leave it at that. The money supply is reasonably measurable; and using it as the prime moving force has a kind of ease of explanation and simplicity that makes it intellectually satisfying. There's no question that the money supply *is* a very important element. But, there are others. Shortages, either real or threatened, and pent-up demand are two of them that have been ignored in our present monetaristic obsession.

The economic history after World War II is well known to most of us. However, let's put it all together to see just where the enormous and recurrent feeding of our inflation tiger came from.

There's not much question that prices really soared whenever an undersupply of much wanted items was threatened. Or, whenever the demand for them exceeded their possible supply. While we are looking at the familiar patterns, let's think about whether there's any nourishment that comes anywhere near the ability of these events to keep the tiger alive.

Pre-Vietnam—Inflation Rose and Then Plateaued

World War II set up the first stage of the inflationary process. It was triggered by a kind of double whammy. Not only was there the effect that most wars have had in creating shortages and escalating prices, but it came after the Great Depression, which had kept living costs unusually low for 10 years. What's more, the war was worldwide and horribly destructive. The productive capacity of all of the industrialized countries of the world was virtually wiped out. The United States was the only exception, and its factory facilities had been used for so long without overhaul that they were pretty worn out. The shortages that were caused by the lack of productive capacity furnished a wonderful breeding ground for inflation.

Savings during the war were enforced, not only by shortages but by rationing of those goods that were available. In addition, most countries had rigidly enforced price controls. It was inevitable that as soon as rationing and price controls were lifted, there was a huge amount of money to spend on both capital and consumer goods. Add to that the pent-up demand which had gone unsatisfied not only during the war, but also during the Great Depression, and there was plenty of reason for the fires of inflation to be lit and burning.

Casualties from the war had decimated the skilled workmen of much of the world and had destroyed a great deal of the wealth of Europe. Americans who were courageous enough to wander around Europe found that they could buy almost anything they wanted—especially land and villas from empoverished owners—at prices that were ridiculously low. But, then came something new and unheard of in the history of warfare. The winners decided to finance the losers as well as their allies. So, instead of keeping Europe in continual poverty, the way back for Germany, Italy, and Japan was surprisingly easy and rapid. The net effect was to increase productive capacity quickly, and to satisfy the pent-up demand and reduce shortages in a relatively short time. That was a counterforce which helped to keep the post-war inflation from lasting too long, or becoming too wild—at least until it received a further upward push later on.

World War II broke up a number of Empires. Countries which had been under the thumb of the Great Powers began to free themselves from the Imperial ties. It took a number of years before the process was completed, but it carried with it the beginnings of the end of cheap, controlled raw material prices. Since many of the OPEC oil producing countries were protectorates of the Great Powers before the war, the break-up of the Imperial groupings was to have very significant long-term inflationary implications.

The labor movement, which had gained some momentum during the Great Depression, had an easy time of it during the post-War period—often with the blessings and encouragement of their Governments. That was the beginning of a sharp escalation in the cost of labor, a powerful element in the prolonged cycle of inflation which followed.

All of these factors led to a rapid increase in prices in the immediate post-War period. Still, in spite of the power of the inflation feeding, few people in the United States were worried. After all, many shortages had been ended and a great deal of demand had been filled. There had been too long a history of economic leveling-offs after previous wars. In fact, there was a general expectation of at least a medium-sized recession after the first thrust of rebuilding. That was reflected in Wall Street, where the fear of an economic downturn was so general that the price/earnings ratio (see Chapter 7) of stocks reached an all-time low.

Perhaps we *would* have had a typical post-war recession, which would have brought the price level down. But, we never had the chance to find out. On June 25, 1950, the Korean War broke out. It took a huge amount of the resources of the United States to fight it, both in manpower and material, and any idea of disinflation was out of the window. Once again, war created shortages and pent-up demand and made President Eisenhower determine to fight the mild inflation which followed with higher interest rates and a modest recession. That was all that was needed to allow for a period of price stability.

It was remarkable that we had won two victories over inflation in spite of two large-scale wars and it seemed obvious that we could begin peace-time economic development without looking over our shoulders to see whether prices were gaining on us. True, we had to accept a *level* of prices significantly higher than those of the 1940s; but, it's the rate of change that counts in inflation fighting. We had made our adjustments and there was no longer any upward momentum. There were some left-over seeds that could germinate, but they would need some fertile soil to spur their growth.

Post-Vietnam—A One-Two-Three Punch

The left-over seeds of inflation were given plenty of fertilizer within a very few years when President Johnson decided that we could afford both guns and butter. By going into debt instead of paying for the Vietnam War as it deepened from a police action into a major conflict, he set the stage for a brand-new inflation.

President Nixon, an economic pragmatist if ever there was one, tried everything in his economic bag of tricks. But even after a series of price controls and a couple of credit crunches, we still had inflation.

There was some hope that the 1974-5 recession might have ended the inflationary push, but it was doomed before it could gain momentum by the aftermath of the Arab oil embargo. When OPEC found that by merely threatening a short supply of oil from time to time it could increase the price at will without fearing a spanking by the Great Powers, it added a new, highly dramatic extra push which shoved prices higher in every industrialized country in the world. It was a new drive toward inflation that continued for years and didn't reach its highest pitch until after the collapse of the Government of the Shah of Iran and the war between Iraq and Iran.

The Rise and Fall of Inflationary Expectations

After the shocks of the Iranian revolution, the Iraq-Iran war, and the Soviet invasion of Afghanistan, it was natural enough that the vast majority of Americans would feel that OPEC would never stop raising prices. What's more, commodity prices soared to astronomical heights. It was a combination that amplified the feeling that prices would never come down. That opinion had been smouldering ever since the first Arab oil boycott, in spite of the pain it caused businessmen who overbuilt inventories just before the 1974-5 recession. By 1980 it was full-blown and provided enough food to keep the inflationary tiger healthy long after it should have begun to lose strength and fade away.

However, inflationary expectations can evaporate as quickly as they begin, and they are doing so now. While there's still an uneasy feeling that prices will go up again if we aren't careful, it isn't backed by reality. In fact, it's really hard to pinpoint many things, except for those that are involved in our military build-up, that can be expected to cost more in the future than they do now. Even more important is the fact that nothing is on the horizon that can supply a major new push toward higher prices. With the factories of the industrialized world operating far below capacity, with a glut of oil, with high unemployment and most demands pretty well satisfied, it will take a great deal to generate any new inflationary momentum. Unless there's a new war, the odds are overwhelming on the side of disinflation. And that's likely to produce more gray hairs than worrying about inflation ever did. The best way to protect yourself against it is to have cash or bonds that can be converted into cash when you want it. At least, that's the first step. Once the disinflationary cycle is fully established those with cash to invest will be in the driver's seat.

Disinflation and its Pain

It's true that prices have gotten progressively higher since the dawn of human civilization, but they go up in cycles rather than in a straight line. Throughout history, there have been periods in which they have gone down and they have been linked to some of the most unpleasant periods of economic life.

Pinpointing the downward cycles of early history is somewhat difficult because much more information is available about kings and military leaders and their battles than about how people lived. We do know something about the *inflationary* times because the leaders often tried to do something about them when they got bad enough.

Diocletian is one example. Prices went up for a long time even after the price-control effort. But they finally broke down as the Roman Empire moved its headquarters eastward, leaving the old frontiers open to barbarian invasion. The isolation of once closely linked communities caused a disintegration into the "Dark Ages" and barter took the place of the money-based trade of the old Empire. Prices certainly declined, but it was also one of the most dismal periods of human history.

Even with the skimpy knowledge we have about Europe after the price escalation caused by the Black Death, it is clear that the fourteenth century was one of the nastiest of the Middle Ages. War-like nobles were able to protect themselves against the decline in the value of their properties back home by forming into marauding groups that preyed on the towns and villages of the middle classes. It was an interesting way to off-set the effects of deflation, and some of the leaders of the knightly companies, such as John Hawkwood, actually became heroes. But, it's hardly a course of action that could be followed in twentieth-century America.

The "Great Price Revolution" of the sixteenth century took its toll when it ended. The seventeenth century is known for its great philosophers and scientists, such as Descartes, Liebnitz, and Galileo. But, it is also known as a century of economic sluggishness and depression.

However, the early record of price disinflation, dismal as it is, doesn't give us precise enough data to enable us to form any sensible investment decisions. To do that, let's go to some of the better documented history of the United States in the nineteenth and twentieth centuries. The record is fascinating because the disinflations of 1837, 1873, 1921, and 1929 bear an eerie resemblance to that which we are now facing.

1837—The Bank War that Caused Depression

Andrew Jackson was not a professional soldier; yet, he became one of the most famous military heroes in the history of the United States. Although he had spent years in politics, he had little of the training in statesmanship with which Thomas Jefferson and the Adams had been imbued. He was a slave owner and a rough-and-ready commander; yet he is regarded as a President who furthered democracy and started the age of the common man. He wasn't a handsome, dashing figure—in fact, he was thin as a rail and plagued with a variety of illnesses; but he never stopped being a heroic figure to Americans, even years after his military triumphs. It's an unusual set of contrasts, but one which has been duplicated often enough by the strange way in which history operates. After all, Julius Caesar didn't become a military man until quite late in life, but he was the most famous general of Rome. Neither was he a dashing figure of a man, but he made such a splash that future Emperors took his name.

However, while President Jackson had a number of strong points, he also had some major weaknesses. The one which stood out most was his lack of understanding of economics. While his most famous battle was undoubtedly his victory in New Orleans, his next biggest fight was against Nicholas Biddle and the Bank of the United States. He won the battle, and reshaped the nation's banking system. But it was far from a triumph! By the time that Van Buren, Jackson's successor, came into office, the United States was in a serious economic mess. Jackson was no longer President, but he had set the stage for the longest depression in our young Republic's life by following a disinflationary course which is hauntingly familiar. He decreased the money supply and raised interest rates just as the demand for goods was falling.

The Economic Climate

By the time Jackson came into office, he was the President of a country which was in the midst of rapid expansion. Bad as the War of 1812 had been, it laid the groundwork for a period of prosperity. The British had mounted a naval blockade which shut us off from a number of European goods. That provided an incentive for domestic industrialization, especially in the northeast. New England built mills which rivaled the output of some of the cotton manufacturing centers of England. Massachusetts had a flourishing shoe and boot industry. Pennsylvania became a center for iron furnaces. The South, meanwhile, opened up new cotton lands and by the 1830s that staple became the nation's leading export commodity.

An equally powerful push came from the new waves of immigrants coming in from Europe. Ever since colonial times, communities had stayed close to the coastline. By the 1820s they were spreading westward. Of course, that put a big strain on the existing means of transportation, which was eased by a large build-up in waterway systems. Besides, the first of the railroads were being built. The Baltimore & Ohio, one of the early roads, had over 1000 miles of track by early in the 1830s.

Canal transport was cheap and efficient. The Erie Canal in New York played a major role. It reduced the cost of transporting goods by up to 80% and opened new territory all the way to the Great Lakes. Population in some of the larger towns along the canals rose by as much as 50% in a short space of time, so other states could not fail to take the Erie as a model for their own development. Pennsylvania built 1000 miles of canals by the mid-1830s and Massachusetts, Virginia, and Maryland were all quick to begin construction of railroads and turnpikes. It was truly a transportation revolution.

The Inflation

It was only inevitable with so many people working on capital improvements such as railroads and canals, and prosperity so widespread, that prices would soon begin to soar. Women working in shops in New England were earning 4 or 5 times as much as their equivalents in Europe. And, as labor was drawn from the farms, crops were smaller and more expensive. Cotton, which accounted for about half of the nation's exports, was in demand and prices were on their way up.

However, the real push of inflation came from speculation. At first it was in the securities of canal companies and railroads, but that was nothing compared to land. The value of real estate in New York doubled in 5 years, and some properties in the Big Apple did far better. Even at that, the increases in the city were nothing compared to those in the newly developed areas. Villages and towns sprang up overnight, and the price of lots increased 2-3 times in less than a year. Public lands were a particularly exciting play. In 1834, less than 5 million acres were sold by the government; by 1836, that total had more than quadrupled to over 20 million acres. Anyone with an inside track to land offices could make a fortune. Land buying companies were formed to buy up public lands and successful speculations made many times their money in short order. With all of that money to be made so easily, land speculation became a popular sport for farmers and merchants as well as financial men. The balloon was blown up, ready to burst and, in 1837, it did!

The Money to Feed the Boom

In the early 1830s a good bit of financing came from England and, to a lesser extent, from the rest of Europe. President Jackson was worried about foreign investment just as some of the more recent Presidents have been. Europe had $200 million invested in our country and could, he said, control our destiny. But, as the boom continued, it was fueled by our own banks, which more than doubled in number over an eight-year period. Their capital kept pace with that figure, but their use of it was more adventurous. The amount of money in circulation more than tripled and loans outstanding quadrupled.

Banking in the United States, especially in some of the newly developed areas, was poorly regulated. And, when the charter of the Bank of the United States was not renewed, the last real chance to control the system was gone. Banks were able to issue their own notes, which became paper currency, so the growth of money in circulation was not restrained by any central authority. Loans were all too often made to favorites of the bank officers, without much regard for their ability to repay. But, the worst offense was in the capital structure. Much of the time the founders who had pledged to buy the stock of the bank didn't do it with cash or gold. Instead, they simply borrowed most of their investment needs from the bank itself. So, a bank with stated capital of about $1 million often had virtually no gold or silver backing for its loans or paper in circulation. The result was a double speculation—a boom built on credit with very little to support it.

Blowing Up the Bubble

The Bank of the United States, with Biddle as its head, was by far the biggest in the United States, with $30 million in capital. It had a quasi-official position. The United States Government bought one-fifth of the stock, while the rest of it was owned by the public. It had 26 branches in the leading cities. In addition to its private depositors, it was the depository for all government funds and, as a consequence, its paper currency was respected in all parts of the country.

President Jackson, suspicious of banks since his youth, felt that too much power was centered in one organization. What's more, he was alarmed by the sizeable foreign ownership of the shares and the rumors that the bank had given donations to the political party which opposed him. He set out to destroy it! The opportunity came when Biddle asked Congress to renew its charter. Congress passed a bill to authorize it, but Jackson vetoed it. As a result of that veto, whether Jackson was aware of it or not, he had lost all control over the soundness of the banking system.

Pumping the Inflation

One of the effects of the demise of the Bank was the loss of a great deal of our overseas backing. British financiers began to look elsewhere in the world for their investment opportunities. While that caused some temporary dislocations at the same time as Biddle, in a fit of pique, decided to contract some of the Bank's operations, the economy was not held down for very long. It was rescued by the expanded credit which President Jackson made possible for other banks to provide. He accomplished that by gradually drawing the government's deposits out of the Bank of United States and placing them with a number of banks around the country, particularly in the west. The officers of those organizations, far less cautious than Biddle, used their new money to the hilt to expand their loans and currency circulation. That increase in the supply of money fueled the last stage of land speculation.

Bursting the Bubble

However, underneath the frothy exterior, the economy was deteriorating. England was having its problems and the demand for cotton for export was slack. A number of the canals and railroads that were being built were not viable economically. Final demand was slipping.

Then, President Jackson committed a cardinal economic sin. With demand for goods fading, he took two steps which had the effect of drying up the money supply:

Always suspicious of paper money, the President decided to refuse to accept it in payment for public land. He demanded specie (gold or silver). Jackson clearly hoped that his demand for payment in metal would diminish land speculation. Instead, its first effect was to throw the banking system into turmoil.

Since most of the new public land sales were taking place in the west, the gold needed to pay for them had to come out of banks of the eastern part of the country. And, to add to the drain, the western banks, trying to get ready for further sales, turned in the paper money they held for redemption in gold by the banks that had issued it. That played havoc in many parts of the country. Some banks in New Orleans were forced to admit that they were simply out of gold. And, in New York and other cities, the yellow metal was hoarded. Banks all over the nation were forced to suspend payment in gold. The eastern banks, drained of their reserves, had to contract their loans and to demand payment from borrowers.

As a result of the sales of government land, the Treasury had piled up a large surplus. President Jackson decided to distribute most of the money to the States. It was still another move to drain gold from the banks which had government funds on deposit.

So the very banks which had been financing industrial development were forced to contract drastically. Failures took place in every part of the commercial complex. Interest rates soared from 7% a year to as high as 2-3% a month. Lower demand for goods *plus* a contracting supply of money was too much for the economic system to take. Bank runs were a frequent occurrence. Unemployment was massive, and most of the jobless were without adequate means of support. Wall Street panicked, as the vast majority of the factories in the eastern states closed down. Finally, the shortage of currency made so much bogus money appear that barter replaced normal trade in many parts of the country. Inflation was over, but it was replaced by disinflation rather than stability. As the price of land and commodities crumbled, fortunes were wiped out.

Of course, the United States recovered and its economy came roaring back some 5 or 6 years later. And that made the disinflation of the depression a wonderful opportunity for those investors who had cash. But how much economic pain could have been avoided if only President Jackson and Nicholas Biddle had been able to get together to avoid the uncalled for expansion and subsequent contraction of the money supply—the latter, just as the economy was already weakening!

The Depression of 1873

Perhaps you are wondering whether our monetary experts in the middle and late 1970s ever took a look at the events of the Jackson era. If so, they certainly had an undue sense of optimism about their ability to avoid the problems that arise if the money supply is pumped up only to be cut back before the economy can get on a firm footing. But, they weren't the only ones in recent years who ignored the lessons of the past. The "experts" who decided how to pay for the Vietnam War didn't give too much attention to the financing of the Civil War which was also accomplished with debt rather than taxes.

It's true that prices went down soon after the Civil War was over. The inflation took place *during* the war, when there were no controls imposed on the civilian economy. Not only was there no great pent-up demand after the Civil War, but there was nothing to push prices higher after it was over. In contrast, after Vietnam was over, the Arab oil boycott gave inflation a big shove forward. Eight years after the War between the States was over, the economy was in deep trouble. Perhaps it's only coincidence that our economy finds itself in hot water after just about the same time span.

Financing the Civil War

At the beginnings of most wars, the leaders like to talk about patriotism, courage, and sacrifice. On the other hand, they are surprisingly shy when it comes to a discussion of how much it is going to cost. World War II was an exception. We knew right at the start that it was going to be a huge effort, and that we would have to pay for it, at least in good part, by very heavy taxes.

When the Civil War broke out on April 12, 1861, the United States was unaccustomed to the massive expenditures it would require. It had a small budget, most of which was paid for by customs duties and tariffs. The national debt was a mere $64 million, but there wasn't any cash in the till. That was solved by a fast bond issue of $8 million, most of it subscribed for by the New York banks. But that kind of money didn't last for long after the fighting started. It was just the beginning of a series of hit-and-miss financings that were to plague the financial system for the duration of the war years.

President Lincoln, who had a very limited financial background, put the nation's financial affairs in the hands of another neophyte, Treasury Secretary Salmon P. Chase, whose picture still appears today on $10,000 bills. He had achieved political prominence by his stand against slavery. Unfortunately, he had a gnawing ambition to become President, which sometimes kept him from taking stands that he knew would be unpopular with the voters. As a result, he was continually underestimating the amount of money the Treasury would need, which forced him to require hurry-up measures to pay the military suppliers and even the troops. In the early days of the war, his official position was that the fighting couldn't last for very long and that there was no need to impose anything as long-lasting as a tax increase. Does that ring any bells about the Vietnam War, over a century later?

However, the southern forces made a great deal of progress soon after the fighting began, and a general financing plan was obviously necessary. Chase's program was as follows:

To impose a tiny tax of 3% on incomes of over $800 a year (which was good pay for 1861).

To raise duties and tariffs, something that the northern industrialists had wanted for some time. Now that the southerners who had opposed higher duties were no longer in Congress, it wasn't difficult to get the vote, even though it imposed a tax on the consumer rather than on the wealthy.

By far the vast majority of the needed funds came from increasing the national debt. As it turned out, the revenues from duties and the income tax were barely enough to pay for the nonmilitary part of the government's expenses. The entire cost of the war itself was financed by debt.

New Tricks of Financing

Well before the end of the first year of the war, Chase had to come up with some unorthodox means of raising money. The southern forces were pulsing further into the Union's territory and Washington itself was in danger. It was a difficult time to persuade potential buyers to open up their purses. The first answer the Treasury came up with was to issue demand notes which were redeemable in gold. At first, military suppliers and troops found them a bit strange, but it wasn't long before they began to accept and use them as though they were money.

Then came a step which was to set the stage for a severe wave of inflation. Chase twisted the arms of the banking system to use its excess reserves of gold to buy $150 million worth of three-year Treasury notes. The theory was that as the gold was paid out, it would find its way back to the banks in the form of deposits. Unfortunately, that didn't happen. Instead, gold was hoarded by a number of people who weren't so sure that their patriotic duty was more important than the preservation of their capital, especially since the struggle threatened to go badly for the Union. With their metal in short supply at the very end of 1861, most banks suspend gold payments; and within a few days the Treasury followed suit. The United States had abandoned the Gold Standard and would not fully return to it for seven years.

Still, gold remained an important metal. Unlike the years following World War II, the dollar wasn't a very important currency in the eyes of the rest of the world and it wasn't acceptable as an international medium of exchange. Gold was needed to settle international obligations, and the United States was a large importer of European merchandise. So, gold began to go to a premium. It started slowly; in the Spring of 1862, the dollar was worth 98 cents, in terms of a unit of gold. By the end of the year, it had declined to a little over 75 cents. From then on, the bear market in the dollar was firmly established, until it reached a low point of about 38 cents in July of 1864. Then, as the Union forces pushed into the South, it began to improve. By the end of the war, it had doubled from its low-water mark and was selling at almost 78 cents.

Paper Money and Bond Drives

During the middle years of the war, while gold was going through the roof, Secretary Chase was adding to the depreciation of the dollar by inventing new ways to increase the national debt. Early in 1862, the first "Legal Tender" act was signed into law. It authorized the issuance of $150 million of United States notes not redeemable in gold, which would be lawful money for payment of everything but duties on imports and interest on the public debt. The notes were a new form of paper currency which were soon known as "Greenbacks." Within a little more than a year, another $300 million worth of Greenbacks were authorized. To that total was added more short-term notes and bonds. Before the war ended, over $440 million worth of Greenbacks were in circulation.

However, selling bonds was like pulling teeth until Chase joined Jay Cooke in October of 1862. That young and aggressive financier persuaded Chase to give him an exclusive on the sale of government bonds, with a commission of ⅜ of 1 percent in the sale of all bonds over the first $10 million. He formed a network of over 2000 salesmen, paying them a part of his fee; and they spread throughout the Union. It was a new approach to selling bonds. Instead of going to the banks and wealthy individuals, this bond drive was aimed at the rank and file. Bonds were distributed anywhere where groups of people could be gotten together—churches, factories, and even army camps. Sales were absolutely astonishing, proving that the appeal to patriotism had much more power when it was directed toward the people than toward the financially conscious rich. That was a lesson that the United States *did* learn from history. The Liberty bond drives of World War II and the E-bond sales of World War II took a page from Jay Cooke's book. His success established him in the ranks of the financiers of the Civil War as well as in the post-war period.

The Effect on Prices

Before the Civil War began, the supply of money in circulation was just short of $700 million. By the time the fighting drew to a close it had more than doubled. Add to that pressure on the price structure the extra expense caused by the gold and tariff-related increase in the cost of imports and the short supply of some of the items used by the troops, and there was every reason for a massive inflation. The total debt of the federal government, starting from a low pre-war level of $65 million, rose a huge 400 times to over $2.6 billion. Price increases started slowly and then took on a head of steam. By the time the war was over, retail prices had more than doubled, with some items such as dry goods and groceries rising even more.

However, once the war was over, the inflationary push ended abruptly. The government stopped spending money, and more than a million men returned to civilian life. The dollar kept improving until it reached near-parity with gold. So, prices began to fall and they continued in a downward path with only some brief interruptions, until the Depression of 1873 sent them sliding even lower.

Aftermath of the War

The South was terribly damaged, but the North had been able to increase both its industrial production and its wealth. Production of such items as iron, lumber, farm implements and woolens were all considerably higher after the war than before it. The net national wealth was over one-third higher. Most important of all, the railroads had piled up huge profits and were ready for a major expansion.

If, as the Reagan Administration believes, putting capital into the hands of corporations and individuals who will invest it is the key to economic expansion, the Civil War certainly did its job. Never before in the history of the United States had there been such aggregations of wealth in the hands of industrialists! Unlike World War II, profiting on the war effort was nothing to be ashamed of. Suppliers to the armed services, many of whom delivered shoddy goods, accumulated fortunes. The low rate of taxation and the inflated prices, only slowly matched by the cost of labor, padded the earnings of manufacturers. Speculators in real estate and collectibles had made huge sums as inflation soared. At the end of the war, there were hundreds of millionaires as opposed to only a handful before the conflict began. And they were ready to spend!

Particularly attractive for new investment were the railroads. For one thing, many of them were able to get large grants of money from the government for construction, under the theory that opening new territories was in the public interest. Cities and towns were quick to support the roads with money, lest they be bypassed in favor of the localities who were willing to bid more. But, the most exciting aspect of the railroads was the huge amount of land that they were given. To insure their right-of-way, some roads received tens of millions of acres—in some cases, up to one-fourth or one-fifth of entire states. For investors, it was a wonderful double play. If they didn't get rich on railroad profits, they could cash in on their land grants. Money poured in not only from those who had been made rich by the War, but also from Europe. Between 1866 and 1873, some 30,000 miles of road were built, almost as much as the total amount that had been in operation before the War.

The Economic Storm

The years immediately following the war were difficult politically because of all of the problems involved in the reconstruction of the South. In spite of that, they were years of great prosperity. Building construction was booming; the farmers were plagued by lower prices, but they managed to keep a step ahead of the sheriff by increasing production; and the railroads were booming. President Grant, although somewhat ineffective, was a friend of big business. And, in Wall Street, things were really hopping. They were days of such great names as Commodore Vanderbilt, Jay Gould, and Jay Cooke (who had demonstrated his ability by his sensational job in selling bonds during the war). There were fights for control of the railroads and struggles for investment banking power. All in all, they were exciting and profitable days.

However, the storm clouds were gathering. Prices and interest rates were moving in opposite directions, a sign that the amount of money available for the economy wasn't growing fast enough to keep prosperity going. In fact, the federal government had been paying off its debt. The amount of all currency in circulation was actually down. That left it up to the banks to supply enough loans to keep the pot boiling. The national banks did what they could by increasing their loans at a far faster clip than the rise in their assets or deposits. But, with a decreasing amount of money in circulation and the gold standard abandoned, it was difficult for the banking system to increase its lendable funds. So, the pace of its lending ability wasn't enough to keep the economic expansion going. Investment from abroad was needed to fill the gap.

Demand in the United States began to fade. The construction industry peaked in 1871. By the following year, the railroads were beginning to show signs of strain. Much of their new mileage had been built simply to take advantage of government lending and land grants. However, even the heavy investment wasn't producing enough earnings. As a result of the consequent waning in interest in railroad securities, a number of them began to borrow short-term money in the hopes that they would soon be able to refinance with longer term debt. Borrowing short term to satisfy long-term financial needs can create liquidity problems if earnings fail to increase. So, the construction programs of the railroads had to slow down because of lack of enough money input.

By early 1873 the United States economy was facing slackening demand from its most important industries and there wasn't enough growth in the money supply to bring it back. All that was needed to start a decline was a shove. And then the economy received a series of downward pushes.

The economies of Europe got into serious difficulties. In May there was a financial crisis in Vienna, which quickly spread to other capitals on the Continent. England's economy had already been softening for some time. Panic hit a number of European stock markets and, in sympathy, the selling spread to American securities that were traded abroad. New money that might have invested in the United States, particularly in the railroads, dried up.

The New York banking system suffered a drain in the late summer and early fall. That was a typical seasonal pattern. Country banks were allowed to keep part of their reserves at money center banks and, since the larger banks in New York paid interest on those bankers' deposits, they received a large amount of money from that source. However, as the crops came in and had to be paid for, the money flowed back to the country banks. Once all of the payments had been made, the funds usually trickled back to New York. But, in 1873, the timing of the flow back to the country banks came at a time when demands for loans for railroads and the stock brokers were getting urgent. Interest rates for short-term money began to rise sharply.

Several important failures in Wall Street triggered off a financial panic. The New York Warehouse and Security Company, an important commercial lender, had made some loans to the Missouri, Kansas, and Texas Railroad which got into serious trouble. So New York Warehouse had to admit its insolvency on September 8, 1873, and it suspended operations. That caused some alarm on Wall Street, and some careful attention to other railroads that were in trouble.

Jay Cooke, the Civil War's financial hero, became the Northern Pacific's financial backer in 1869. He did a good job in promoting the railroad, and in selling bonds. But the railroad had a number of unplanned difficulties, such as washed-out roadbeds and bridges that collapsed. It needed more money, but couldn't sell a new bond issue. That so weakened the finances of Cooke's firm that it was forced to close its doors on September 18. Cooke's failure really shook Wall Street.

With the stock market crumbling, the shortages of funds in the New York banks really began to have its effect. Call money went from .5% to 1% a *day*. Runs began to develop at a number of banks as questions arose about their financial soundness. Now, the fat was really in the fire. The Stock Exchange, for the first time in its history, shut down trading from September 20 to September 30.

President Grant and Treasury Secretary Richardson arrived in New York on September 20 to try to help out. By then, large amounts of currency had been pulled out of the banks and had gone into hiding. A number of financial people asked the President to deposit $20 to $40 million in a number of money center banks to calm the financial community. But, all that President Grant was willing to do was to buy government bonds from the banks, which was expected to have an effect similar to that of injecting new cash. Unfortunately, most of the bonds were in the hands of the savings banks, and little of the new money reached the commercial banks which needed it. President Grant, with his limited financial experience, wasn't particularly alarmed by the situation, which he felt would do much more harm to speculators than to the nation as a whole.

Unable to get enough money together, a number of banks collapsed. New York's problems spread to other parts of the country, and in some areas the shortage of currency became so acute that banks were paralyzed and barter replaced cash transactions. Young as the Depression was, it already had the force of a financial hurricane.

How Bad was the Depression?

The slump in business lasted, with minor interruptions, from 1873 to 1879. The damage in that six-year period was not to be exceeded until the Great Depression of the 1930s. Business activity declined by over 30%. Mills and factories closed by the scores and unemployment in some eastern states hit one-fourth to one-third of the work force. Unemployment figures weren't too accurate in the 1870s, but it was commonly believed that as many as 3 million people were out of work, out of a population of only about 43 million and an estimated work force of about 15 million. Bankruptcies were widespread.

Of course, prices fell sharply. Wholesale commodities plunged by as much as 30%. But, disinflation, when it comes in this kind of package, is just too rough for anyone to be willing to handle!

1982 and 1873—Some Similarities

In 1873, final demand had been slack for some time before the real downturn began; that is also true in 1982. The early signs of weakness then were in the most important industries—buildings and transportation; now, the same thing can be said, substituting automobiles for railroads. Then, farm prices had been weak, and the farmer was barely able to keep his head above water by producing large crops; that's also true in 1982. Then, foreign financing was extremely important, but its flow stopped because of economic difficulties abroad; now, OPEC has suffered sharp reversals, and instead of being a huge lender to our banking system, and those of other industrialized countries, it has actually become a net borrower. Then the railroads were suffering from a liquidity problem because they had difficulty borrowing long term and were forced to resort to short-term money; now, that's true for many segments of American industry. Then, it was up to the banks to lend enough money to keep the economic pot boiling! But when they were confronted with withdrawals of deposits, and uncollectible loans, they were unable to do the job. In 1982, the savings banks are suffering from a massive withdrawal of deposits. The money center banks seem to be sound, but they have made such a large amount of uncollectible loans to individuals, corporations, and above all to foreign governments such as Poland, Rumania and the less-developed countries, that it is difficult to be sure of just how secure they really are.

Of course, there are differences as well. The Federal Reserve and FDIC are around to help the banks in the event of emergency. The Federal budget is going up rather than down. And the tax cuts are intended to give a boost to demands. These things should help to soften the downward trend and to keep the economy from falling into a hole as deep and long as that of 1873. But, let's hope that President Reagan and his economists have an eye on the similarity between the forces at work, as well as the differences, because anything close to the 1873 experience could hardly be tolerated now without causing great damage to the entire fabric of our society.

1920—Record Price Declines

In the summer of 1920, the economy slid into a Depression. It was over by 1922, making it a particularly short downturn. But, it was noteworthy because it brought about the sharpest price decline in United States history. Wholesale prices declined 45%, and while retail prices were nowhere near as weak, they fell by 12–13%. Unemployment reached a level of over 4,700,000 and business failures were plentiful.

The Aftermath of World War I

By the time the War to end all wars was over, the United States had the only industrial complex that was intact. In fact, it was almost too strong. The Wilson Administration had planned for a war that would last considerably longer. So, it was in a great hurry to cancel its war production contracts. Within a little more than a month, military producers had lost well over $2 billion worth of contracts. There hadn't been much planning about what to do once an Armistice was declared, so the demobilization of men and facilities was pretty sloppy. War time controls, and the bureaucrats who had administered them rather well, were mustered out rapidly. As a result of the cancellation of war-time orders, production fell off, returning troops were slow to find jobs and unemployment mounted. But, that slowdown lasted only through the winter of 1918–19, after which a sharp recovery began.

The Post-War Inflation

The United States hadn't suffered from very many shortages of consumer goods even when roughly one-fourth of the nation's production was dedicated to the war effort. However, a number of *durable* goods had been in short supply, and the pent-up demand for automobiles, furniture, and housing started a boom in the industries which supplied them. Manufacturers also needed capital equipment to convert their factories from war-time to peace-time production and Europe needed almost everything we could give it. By the third quarter of 1919, the whole economy was moving forward rapidly. Production was nearly 20% higher than it had been in 1914.

While this increase of demand was taking place, the Federal Reserve was being accommodating. The government made loans to Europe and, in addition, it had some hangover involvement in such things as ship building and railroad modernization. So, it was still in the market to borrow money. The Federal Reserve aided by keeping interest rates artificially low and permitting the money stock to expand until late in 1919.

Naturally, this combination of demand and low-interest rates caused prices to rise. There had been a surge of inflation during the war, when prices rose between 10–15% a year. After 1919, the inflationary trend accelerated. By June 1920, prices passed their war-time peak by some 25%.

The Downturn Begins

Late in 1919, months before the inflationary peak was over, the Federal Reserve reversed itself, and began to contract the supply of money. It started slowly, but moved with increasing speed as the months went by. Meanwhile, early in 1920, the United States curtailed its loans to Europe, except for money it had to lend some countries so that they would keep their interest payments current. (That strangely gentle way of dealing with debtors is being duplicated with a vengeance in 1982.) Since the United States government no longer needed to raise money, the Federal Reserve was free to worry about inflation. It raised its discount rate from 4.75% to 5.5% late in 1919, and didn't stop increasing it until it had reached 7%. Notes in circulation began to decrease, and the monetary squeeze was on! The money stock was cut by 9% from 1920 to 1921.

However, inflationary expectations were high in 1919 and early 1920. They were reflected in a land boom and in a rapid accumulation of inventories by businessmen. In spite of the fact that final demand wasn't very powerful after the earlier thrust into capital goods and housing, inventories rose to over double the normal level for that era, much of it financed by bank credit. Mortgages outstanding rose to over double the pre-war level and farmers were deeply in hock.

The combination of slack demand, high debt, and a contracting money stock caused a rush to dispose of inventories, an epidemic of bank failures, and sharply lower prices on Wall Street. And the sharpest decline in prices in United States history!

However, the decline in prices and a more relaxed monetary policy laid the groundwork for a noninflationary expansion which lasted until 1929. Perhaps that kind of short economic contraction, although painful, would be a good present day alternative!

1929—What a Price to Pay for Disinflation!

So much has been said about the Great Depression that there's not much point in going into any great detail about it. However, it was a time of sharp declines in prices of all kinds. The money value of the nation's output dropped 46% and unemployment reached the 25% level. As President Roosevelt said, one-third of the nation was underclothed, underhoused and underfed. It was an experience that no one wants to see repeated, and today's politicians should have more than enough ammunition to prevent anything even close to the collapse that occurred.

Interestingly enough, monetary policy was quite restrained during most of the late 1920s. Inflation was no problem, nor was credit restraint. Final demand, however, had begun to weaken some time before the stock market crash. A real estate and housing boom that began after the recovery in 1922 lost its steam back in 1926. Wages rose only moderately and commodity prices actually fell between 1926 and 1929. Almost all of the excitement was in the stock market!

Wall Street was the scene of the wildest kind of speculation, much of it on credit. Customers' margins in their accounts with brokers were pitifully inadequate, and the banks, and even some corporations, were financing the brokers. By mid-1929, stocks were selling so far above anything that they could possibly be worth, that there were miles of blue sky between their prices and reality. And, all of that crazy speculation was built on a mountain of debt.

You can guess what happened! The Federal Reserve took its eye off the not-so-dramatic slippage of demand, and began to watch Wall Street. Credit was tightened, and call money went to 20% and more. For some time it wasn't

enough to stop the market, but it *did* put a further crimp in
business activity. Then, abruptly, came the greatest crash
in Wall Street's history.

Even after the crash, business didn't collapse immediately. It was during that period that the Federal Reserve
made its greatest error by failing to change its direction
and by not bailing out the first banks to go under. The stock
of money fell by over one-third between its peak in August
1929 and its low point in March 1933. That was over three
times as large a plunge as those of any other periods in
United States history. Unquestionably, that increased and
prolonged the agony unnecessarily.

Conclusion

President Hoover told the nation that "prosperity is just
around the corner" even as the breadlines were growing
longer and longer and the financial structure was collaps-
ing. President Grant regarded the financial panic of his
time as nasty for the speculators, but good for the nation.
Now, President Reagan has been assuring us for some time
that recovery is close at hand. All of these men have undeni-
able talents—they need them to be elected President of the
United States. But, they could never have held down jobs
as forecasters!

It's too bad that our political leaders feel that they must
present an optimistic front, no matter what. If they would
be realistic instead, they could give the business and financial communities a great deal of help in establishing their
plans for the future. There's such a vast amount of information available to Presidents that nothing could be more
constructive than to have them tell the truth. Presidential
credibility on economic affairs is, after all, more important
than scarcely believable optimism.

Similarities of Past Business Slumps

In addition to Presidential bullishness, which has been a
common element in most of the downturns, there are a
number of common threads that run through them:

Final demand began to weaken some time before any real crisis was visible. Usually, that lack of strength was disguised by some kind of excitement that commanded much more attention than the less noticeable weakness in demand. Such things as wild speculation in real estate, or in Wall Street, or in inventory were far more visible.

The monetary authorities tended to ignore the developing weakness and focus in on the more frothy, exciting action. They then set out to control it by tightening up on the monetary reins, either consciously or, at times, with some theoretical notion in mind. Usually, their timing couldn't have been worse.

The banking systems and the financiers were overextended with loans to the areas of the economy that have been most exciting. A combination of a fading underlying economy and monetary tightness caused defaults on large loans, leading to a number of financial failures.

Usually, the result has been panic. The President and the monetary authorities have been slow to act, and it's led to depressions. Prices came down, but the cost has been terrible.

What About Now?

Undoubtedly, the present economic environment bears significant similarities to the bad old days. If history is any guide, we've made a number of the same mistakes that have caused so much trouble in the past. And, our present disinflationary trend can easily slip over into a really serious economic decline. Let's look at some of the patterns that resemble those of the past.

Final demand has been deteriorating for some time. Otherwise, our factories would not be operating at only 70% of capacity. Nor, would commodity and raw material prices have suffered a plunge that rivals some of the worst ones in history. It's true that the slide in productivity and the high cost of distribution has kept the slump in raw material prices from being passed along to the ultimate user—as yet. The cost of living is still rising, although at a much reduced rate. But, since there's no sign of a build up in demand, consumer prices should begin to join raw materials on their way down.

Paul Volker's Federal Reserve has been stringent, in spite of the weakness of the economy. While high interest rates may be responsible for some of the slowdown of autos and housing, it's far from certain that lowering them somewhat will produce any great pick up in the economy as a whole. It's widely believed that as prices decline demand will increase, but history shows that there may be a considerable time lag before that happens. Besides, interest rates will probably decline, but they will slide to normal levels only as economy becomes much weaker.

Let's not be fooled by the fact that there doesn't seem to be any wild speculation in land or in Wall Street or in inventories. Because, we have our own special exaggeration that has commanded, and will continue to command everyone's attention. It's credit! Almost everything in our economic life—from the consumer to our largest corporations—is floating on a sea of debt. As a result, liquidity is at a pitifully low level, and there is a whole raft of debt that won't be paid off on schedule—if ever. Besides, there's an extremely dangerous area that can potentially do very great damage. It's home prices! If they begin to slide sharply, our banks can be stuck with a colossal amount of failing mortgages. Monetary restraint at a time when everyone is heavily in debt is terribly risky.

At any other time in our economic history the banking system would have already suffered a deep crisis. So far, our safety measures have been able to keep major problems from surfacing, but can they continue to do so indefinitely? Savings banks all over the country are in trouble. Our money center banks have billions of dollars worth of loans that can't be paid off. Such huge corporations as Chrysler and International Harvester have been rescued, but the next ones may be more difficult to deal with. Huge foreign loans that are in default have simply been extended. And the Federal Deposit Insurance Corporation has performed heroically in pushing failing savings banks into stronger hands. As the economies of the world deteriorate, the need for rescue efforts will become greater and greater.

By definition, it's impossible to predict an accident. But, it *is* possible to know when the risk of accident is great. And, our banking system is certainly accident-prone. Remember, that most of the nasty economic events of the past have had a banking panic before they became really bad!

The Message for Investors

It's a good time to hold on to cash. At least until the danger is over or the potential crisis has struck. Once the smoke has cleared, there will be a number of ways to make money. The first will be in the bond market. It presents one of those either/or potentials. *Either* interest rates must come down moderately if we are going to have any economic recovery at all. *Or*, if they don't go lower soon, we will slide into a much deeper recession and that will eventually drive interest rates down very sharply.

After the surge in the bond market, the second great opportunity will be in common stocks, which should then be selling at historically low levels. We'll talk about both markets in the following chapters.

CHAPTER 6

Making Money in the Bond Market

I think that the first place to make a great deal of money will be in the bond market. (Remember that bonds go *up* as interest rates go *down* and vice-versa.) However, there are many people who don't agree with me. That's the kind of disagreement which can make for the best profit opportunities. But, before you decide to make any investment, you should appraise the negatives as well as the positives. In the case of bonds, the positive side is the price at which they *should* be selling, if they were valued according to traditional standards. The negative side is the supply–demand situation which, according to some experts, will actually make bonds go down rather than up. I am convinced that value will win out. But, let's take a look at the two opposing views.

Positive—The Valuation of Bonds

Historically, the interest rates that you should receive from bonds is made up of two factors:

Payment for the use of your money if there is no inflation to consider—the so-called *real* interest rate, as distinguished from the *nominal* rate which does include the premium you would expect to make up for the diminished purchasing power that inflation would cause. *Real* interest rates have varied considerably. During the last 20 years, they have even been on the minus side from time to time. But overall, they are usually figured to be about 2% for government bonds and a percent or so higher for corporate bonds of the best quality. To that percentage, you must add the *anticipated* rate of inflation, which has varied all over the place.

The Reason for the Inflation Premium

Just suppose that you were being paid off now for $100 worth of bonds in which you'd invested sometime in the 1950s. Then you could have had a few fancy dinners at some good restaurant for $100. Now, it would barely get you out of the grocery store. True, you would have gotten interest on your money throughout the years, but it would have hardly repaid you for the loss in buying power you would have suffered. Only if the annual interest payments were very high would they have paid you back for the shrinking value of the amount of money you had invested.

Increase that $100 to billions of dollars, and you get an idea of how much inflation has cost the owners of long-term bonds. And just to make things worse, interest rates were very low years back, when the bonds were bought. Long-term governments paid less than 3% until 1955, and didn't climb to over 6% until 1969—a far cry from the 14% which they fetched in 1982. No wonder the traditional users of long-term bonds, such as the pension funds, banks, and insurance companies are gun-shy. Instead of being conservative bond buyers, they should have invested in stocks or real estate. If they were at all careful, they would have lost far less of their purchasing power than they did. Now that it is too late, a number of them have decided to divert large amounts of money into real estate and even collectibles. Their timing is probably bad once again, because real estate and collectibles are very risky in a disinflationary environment. But even with yields very high, some money is being switched away from the bond market.

An even more dramatic case in point is what's happening to the savings banks. They loaned huge amounts of money on mortgages, much of it at the low rates of interest that prevailed years ago. Now, to keep a flow of money coming into the banks, they have to pay much higher rates than they are getting back from their old loans. It's a little like a manufacturer who has committed to sell his products at a price which is now below his raw material costs. No wonder so many savings banks are in trouble! It's a real lesson about how expensive it can be to underestimate the inflation premium a lender should get!

What Premium Should be Paid for Inflation?

Obviously, the bond market watches the monthly inflation figures like a hawk, to see whether it is in line with the expectations of the economists who try to forecast it. Any variation from the forecasts is carefully examined to see whether it should imply a change in the expectation of what future rates will be. Even though the monthly figure can be influenced by temporary events, such as the effect of poor weather on food prices, it is a major input for what really counts—*inflationary expectations*. But they are not always the same as the current figure. For example, in 1982 even the Administration's economists are afraid to be too optimistic. They tell us that the inflation rate must rise again to about 7% for the full year. That would be an improvement from 1981s figures, but nothing much to cheer about. I believe that it will turn out to be substantially lower.

The Value of Bonds

Now, let's apply the formula by adding the inflation-premium figure to 2-3% *real* interest for the use of money. If the Administration's inflation forecast is correct, government bonds should be selling to yield 9% rather than the nearly 14% they fetch now. That would mean a 25-30% advance in price. And, if disinflation is the order of the day in spite of the caution of Reagan's economists, the profit would be much larger. It would be the equivalent of the Dow Jones Stock Average going to 2000—clearly, a once-in-a lifetime opportunity. But, let's see what can interfere with that opportunity.

Negative—Demand-Supply

Like everything in economics, price isn't determined by value alone. If there's more supply of anything than the money available to buy it, prices will decline. That's the problem confronting the bond market right now. The main culprit that is likely to do damage to the supply-demand equation is the government's deficit which must be financed by a huge amount of Treasury bills, notes, and bonds.

The deficit has been a growing disappointment. President Reagan came into office pledging to reduce the deficit gradually until it would come into balance by the end of his term in office. The bond market was skeptical about that, but it hoped that he could do it. Instead:

The recession greatly reduced revenues.
Defense spending will be higher than we dreamed.
Congress has dragged its heels about some of the spending cuts the President proposed. As a result, we are looking at back-to-back deficits of $100 billion—and some pessimists think that it will be even more than that.

Usually even that tremendous sum of money could be raised with only a moderate amount of difficulty. But the huge federal deficit comes at a time when there is a tremendous liquidity squeeze throughout our entire economic structure. Corporations have spent years wrestling with high interest rates, always hoping that they would decline sooner or later. So, they have borrowed short term rather than floating long-term bonds, waiting for the opportunity to switch from the short term to the long term when rates would be down. Unfortunately, except for a few months when the Federal Reserve has eased a little, they've never had the chance. A few of our stronger companies have taken advantage of those brief periods of time, but most corporations couldn't get to the market quickly enough. Besides, the preference of bond buyers was overwhelmingly for the strongest corporations and they weren't willing to put up their money for even some very good, smaller companies, even though they could have earned higher interest rates.

The result is that a large percentage of corporate America is borrowing from the banks or from the commercial paper market. That's a very uncomfortable situation, because many of the loans are payable on demand, or must be renewed regularly at fluctuating interest rates. If the amount of money available in the banking system should dry up, there could be a wild scramble for funds. How can business plan its long-term future with the continual financing cloud hanging over their heads?

This situation has given rise to a theory of which Henry Kaufman of Salomon Brothers is the leading spokesman. It's that the government will be able to place its bonds and notes, no matter how large the quantity. But the amount of its placements will be so great and will take so much of the money that is available for fixed-income investment, that there won't be enough left over for corporate borrowers. Rates may come down for a while, but that will cause a rush by corporations to sell billions and billions of dollars worth of long-term bonds. They won't all be able to do so unless there's a considerable easing in the monetary situation because there's a pecking order in the bond market. American Telephone bonds and some industrial grants will be able to float issues. But most companies, on a lower scale of the pecking order, will either have to wait or they will have to pay higher rates.

So, the "crowding-out" theory says that even if interest rates may come down a bit, the Treasury financing will muscle corporations out of the bond market. It won't be so bad as long as the economy stays weak. But when it begins to recover, the demand for money will increase and it will only be available at higher rates.

The die is cast, according to the "crowding-out" theory. Either the recession will become deeper or any mild recovery will once again start interest rates up to the point where they will cause another downturn. In the meanwhile, there's no point in buying long-term bonds unless you are prepared to sell them quickly while the recession-induced decline is still going on. It's a theory that has a great many believers, and it has kept the bond market from having the gains it should have been able to realize from the decline in the inflation rate.

Reasons for Choosing the Positive Side

Powerful as the "crowding-out" theory seems to be, I think that there is no question that bonds will go up to a price approximating their valuation. My reasons are as follows:

The "crowding-out" theory presupposes that the economy will improve for longer than a temporary blip. But, it won't. It will take a long time before it begins to get better. In the meantime, inventories will be cut back and stay at a low level, which will allow many corporations to pay down their short-term debt. Consumers will borrow less as they cut back their purchases, many of which were made because they expected inflation to continue. Capital spending will slow to a walk, as companies worry about how to improve the utilization of their existing plants rather than thinking about new ones. As a result, borrowing demands will begin to decline, and the banks will have more money to lend. As they begin to compete for loans, interest rates will go down. That is the course of events which has happened in all of the previous recessions in the history of the United States, and there's no reason to think that it will be different now.

The tax cuts will spur savings rather than a new wave of buying. The IRAs and other props to encourage Americans to salt away money, will create plenty of new funds for investments.

The continuing dip in inflation will pick up believers. As the conviction that inflation has been replaced by disinflation grows, money will crawl out of unexpected sources to pile into the bond market. The huge difference between the valuation of bonds and their selling prices will be too tasty to ignore.

As disinflation demonstrates its staying power, the Federal Reserve will be able to turn its attention away from inflation-fighting and direct it to helping the economy. Its effort in that direction may be a little late and a little too gingerly at first, but it will help to ease the demand–supply problem and encourage those who will be able to count on continued monetary easing. In fact, the Federal Reserve may not have a difficult time of it. As loan demand evaporates, the money supply will automatically go down. So monetary easing will be possible within the stated goals of money supply increases.

As short-term rates decline, money will flow out of the money funds into higher yielding notes and bonds. There's enough stashed away in those funds to handle the supply problem easily.

Before the budget struggle is over, we'll probably see some higher taxes. That should make the outlook for future Treasury debt financing much brighter.

So, I think that the odds are as good as you will ever see them, when you're dealing in securities markets, that the bond market will soar to near its true valuation level. The payoff will be large enough to please anyone. All you have to do is to choose the area of the fixed-issue market that suits you best, and start investing in it.

To get an idea of the potential investment areas, let's look at how the bond market has changed into what it is today, and then at the various market segments that are available.

The Modern Bond Market and its Origin

For most of its history, the bond market existed simply to serve the wealthy. They bought fixed-income securities so that they could live on a secured income. Young men from Ivy League colleges, who were socially well-connected, could make a living by selling bonds to their rich friends and their families. *Who* they knew was far more important than *what* they knew. The first shock came during the Great Depression, when so many once well-regarded companies were forced into bankruptcy that it became important to know something about credit risks. But, for the most part, the bond market remained a social club, without the fascination of the large and rapid fluctuations that took place in the stock market. Many of us still have the feeling that bonds don't offer much of a chance to make a lot of money, except for those who have millions to play with. That's just a hangover from the old, bygone days. Now, nothing could be further from the truth!

The modern bond market fluctuates with even more violence than the stock market. Fixed-income securities can be carried on very low margin, and for those who really want to speculate there are extremely active futures and options markets that permit investors to control large amounts of bonds with very little money. Furthermore, it is no longer a sleepy social club. Instead, it is full of some of the brightest, most aggressive people in all of Wall Street.

How the Transformation took Place

Why the enormous change? It all began when pension fund, insurance company, and bank portfolio people discovered that by managing their positions aggressively, they could improve them. They began to take advantage of small changes in the market to swap one bond for another in order to upgrade the quality of their holdings or to improve their yields. Each individual improvement was small. For example, suppose that there was a buyer of bonds in one of the subsidiaries of American Telephone which Fund X owned, while there was a seller in another, equally well-secured bond of another AT&T subsidiary. By selling the bonds it owned and swapping them into the ones that were for sale, Fund X could improve its yield by a small fraction of 1%. That, in itself, was not very significant. But, if it continued this "swapping" very actively, after some time had passed, its yield from the bond portfolio could be measurably better. Since Fund X had hundreds of millions of dollars worth of bonds, the improvement was well worth the time and effort.

However, bond "swapping" isn't simple. The people at the trading desk of the funds and at their brokers have to perform complicated calculations involving compound interest and the relation of price and yields to the number of years that the bonds still have left until they are scheduled to be paid off. And the traders must have those calculations performed very quickly. Clearly, that calls for computers! So a new breed of bond man is needed. He must know mathematics, be able to work with computers and their programmers, and be ready to make snap decisions about moving large quantities of bonds. Out went the Ivy League socialites! In came a new group of people who were ready to launch the most creative and speculative area of Wall Street.

The Federal Reserve Becomes More Aggressive

Of course, the Federal Reserve had always been the most important single factor in the determination of interest rates. Its policy was previously based on the idea that it should correct unusual economic events, so its actions followed broad patterns that took some time to develop. Once tuned onto the Fed policy, it could be followed for a rather long stretch of time.

However, by the early 1970s it became obvious to economic policy makers that the Fed was the main tool that could be used in the fight against inflation—or, if need be, against recession. So, time after time, it would tighten the monetary reins, only to loosen them abruptly if the economy began to suffer. It also began to engage in frequent mid-course corrections. Often, that made for several large up and down see-saws in interest rates within the space of a year.

The violence of those fluctuations increased in the late 1970s and early 1980s. By now, trying to guess what the Fed is going to do next is one of the most fascinating sports in Wall Street. As money-market "experts" try to *anticipate* future Fed actions, there are frequently large fluctuations in the bond market that are often unrelated to any actual changes in monetary policy. A perfect example is the Friday afternoon drama that comes after the release of the weekly money supply figures. Often those figures show temporary movements that will be undone within a few weeks. But, they can cause large changes in bond prices.

The excitement of the quick changes in interest rates gave some of the bright newcomers to the bond market a fresh idea. Since the ability to make gains (or losses) on bonds was just as important as clipping coupons, why not develop a way to consider only the fluctuations and ignore interest payments. So, a number of Exchanges decided to allow organized trading in futures and options, which entitle the buyers or sellers to take advantage of changes in the price of fixed-income securities without getting any of the interest payments. That inaugurated some of the fastest-growing trading markets in existence.

Now that there are a number of ways to speculate in short- or medium-term price movements, money-market traders really focus in on the economic data that are released regularly by various divisions of the government. Let's take a look at some of the reports that they follow as carefully as though they were thermometers measuring the temperature of the economy.

The Consumer Price Index (CPI)

The Consumer Price Index has assumed such importance in our economic life that you would think that investigators polled a huge number of stores and selling outlets all over the country to find out how much things cost. Not at all! Less than 25,000 selling outlets and hospitals are asked about the prices of under 400 items every month. The final figure is a weighted average of items, including food, medical care, apparel, and other goods. The resultant average is then compared to that of the month before and the difference between them is reported.

However, the CPI doesn't give a realistic idea of changes in the cost of living. The reason is that it is so heavily weighted by the cost of housing, which comprises 48.5% of the index. While it is true that the cost of housing is the biggest single item in the budget of most Americans, it actually doesn't change much from month to month, except for the relatively few people who move or buy homes. Still, the CPI includes changes in mortgage rates and in the price of homes. As a result, the final figure receives a powerful upward push whenever interest rates go up, although the vast majority of homeowners don't really experience any change at all. The CPI is unrealistically boosted in an inflationary environment and lowered in a disinflationary one. Our government economists are aware of the tendency toward distortion, and less emphasis will be given to the housing sector—but not until 1983.

Still another distortion comes from the fact that at times of disinflation a number of price reductions aren't recorded. Some official discounts, such as those current in the automobile industry, do get into the figure, but privately negotiated discounts do not. Nonetheless, although it's not the most reliable index of inflation we could have, the bond market pays very close attention to the CPI. When it comes out near the end of each month, it is responsible not only for large see-saw moves in fixed-income securities, but also for changes in bond buyer attitudes.

Producer Price Index (PPI)

This measure of wholesale prices comes out in the first week or so of every month. It is an attempt to measure the movement of prices before they reach the consumer, and it is considered a forerunner of CPIs of the future. There are three segments that go into making up the PPI.

1. Crude materials, such as agricultural products, petroleum and scrap metals.

2. Intermediate goods, including such things as paper boxes, mill products, auto parts and other equipment.

3. Finished goods, such as farm equipment, and food and clothing before they are sold to retailers.

The PPI receives less attention than the CPI, although it is actually the more reliable indicator of the *future* direction of inflation.

Unemployment

Early every month, we get the unemployment report. It really has an impact! It makes waves in Congress, and there is a general impression that it will influence the Federal Reserve. If unemployment becomes too high, the reasoning goes, the Fed will be afraid to stay tough; on the other hand, if it shrinks, a firmer stance can be taken.

Actually, we don't get a real count of the unemployed. The figure is compiled from a poll of some 60,000 households taken in the week that contains the 12th day of the month before. So, by the time we get the report in a rapidly changing economy, it can be pretty old stuff. A more up-to-date idea of what's going on can be gathered from newspaper reports about layoffs or rehirings.

There's one important distortion in the unemployment report. It is in the count of so-called "discouraged workers." When people decide that there's no point in looking for work any more, because there aren't any jobs to be had, they are no longer considered to be in the ranks of the unemployed. Really, that doesn't make much sense, because they represent one of the worst problems in a recession, and should be counted in the total figure in some way. Right now, for example, "discouraged workers" would make the count of unemployed as much as 3% higher than that which is reported to us. Still another distortion comes from the number of people who are working part-time instead of full-time.

In spite of the inaccuracies of the unemployment report, it is the most important indicator of all, and its effect on bond prices can be longer lasting than the others.

The Leading Indicators

There are 12 segments of the economy that have been chosen to predict the strength or weakness of business activity in the months to come. Some of the things considered are: inventories on hand; crude material prices; liquid assets; stock prices; and the money supply. The Commerce Department calculates the changes in each of them from the month before and totals them to form an index which it reports on the last few days of each month.

It's generally considered that if the "leading indicators" decline for three months in a row, it's a warning signal that a recession is coming. However, that hasn't always been true in the past, so the "leading indicators" have lost some of their magic. One reason is that it sometimes includes data that have worked at other times, but just aren't appropriate for present conditions. For example, one of the segments considered is the money supply. Usually, if it goes up, easier credit conditions will follow reasonably quickly. But, when the Fed is pledged to a stringent monetary policy, as it is now, it's completely the other way around. On the one hand, if the money supply expands, it means that the Fed may soon start to tighten, and that interest rates will go higher, not lower. On the other hand, a declining money supply can put the Fed in a position to let interest rates fall. So, until the Fed changes its policy, an increase in the money supply should be considered as unfavorable, rather than favorable as the "leading indicators" would have it.

The Money Supply

A great deal of controversy rages about how broadly based the money supply figure should be. The one that gets most attention is M-1, which is intended to include only the amount of money that is readily available for spending. It is made up of the total of currency in circulation, and checking deposits, both interest-bearing and noninterest-bearing, and the Fed reports the change in the number each Friday afternoon. However, it ignores such huge sums as those in the money market funds, which have risen from a standing start to the point where they are approaching the $200 billion level. A good bit of that money *could* be readily available for spending, so it is a distortion to ignore it. Actually, the amount of money in those funds is reported each week by private economists, but not by the Fed, which simply includes it once a month when it reports the M-2 figure.

The weekly M-1 figure makes a big splash in the over-the-counter bond market every Friday afternoon, after trading on the Exchange is closed. Naturally, its effect carries over to the Exchanges on Monday. However, intermediate and long-term investors should take it with a grain of salt. It is often influenced by one-shot events such as large Social Security or tax refund payments, international flows of money, or even the weather. So, sometimes it takes a big jump that has no real influence on the longer term. If Fed policy hasn't changed, chances are that any bulges will be wiped out within a month or two. So, don't take those one- or two-week discrepancies too seriously!

In fact, the Fed itself is considering a change in its reports. It may soon give a 4-week average money supply figure rather than a weekly number. Of course, that won't stop private money market watchers from making their own estimates about the weekly changes. That's likely to make the Friday afternoon scramble even more unreliable than ever! Why doesn't the Fed decide to join the modern trend toward full disclosure and give us *more* information rather than *less*?

How to Invest in the Bond Market

Even if you agree with me that bonds have nowhere to go but up, except for an occasional interruption when one of those economic reports we've talked about scares the market temporarily, you can't stop there. You must choose the right area in which to invest. It must be one that fits both your purse and your temperament. You can put your money to work in a wide spectrum of market areas, ranging from the ultraconservative to the highly speculative. Naturally, you'll receive much more "bang from your bucks" the more speculative you become. But unless you are prepared to spend the time to follow short-term fluctuations, you shouldn't invest in anything that swings as wildly as the futures market. In that case, you might want to choose something in between the conservative and the swinging markets. Let's examine some of the possibilities.

Treasury Bills

Every week there is an auction of Treasury Bills which will be repaid 3, 6, or 12 months from the time you buy them. It's a true auction, which accepts bids from professionals, like banks, and averages them to arrive at the rate which individual investors will receive. The rate at each auction varies with the ups and downs of the short-term interest rates.

T-Bills are unquestionably the safest investment possible, because they will be paid off even if the government has to print the money. So, if you hold them to maturity, the only risk is that in an inflationary environment the dollars you get back will be worth a little less. T-Bills have some major advantages, in addition to their safety. The interest you receive is subject to federal taxes, but not to local or state taxes. But, interest may not be the proper word. Actually, instead of paying as they go, T-Bills are sold at a discount and you collect the *equivalent* of interest in the form of the difference between what you paid and the 100 cents on a dollar that will be returned to you. For example, if you paid $900 for a one-year T-bill with a face value of $1000, you'd have made $100 on your $900 investment, instead of getting checks for interest. You can sell the bills before they mature, if you want. There's a regular market which fluctuates with the daily changes in interest rates.

T-bills can be bought on very slim margin, if you want. And there is a futures market for them. But, if you want to pay for them in full, they are an absolutely safe place in which you can earn something when you are parking your money while you are waiting to decide what to do with it.

Treasury Notes

One of the most popular issues of governments are treasury notes which mature in from one to seven years. They have great appeal to those investors who want to have the safety of a Treasury issue while they stay in the increasingly popular mid-range of maturities. Fears about future inflation rates have made buyers decide to own these intermediate-term bonds rather than to worry about what the purchasing power of the dollar will be 20 or 30 years from now.

Treasury notes pay interest semi-annually, and their prices are reported each day in the financial pages of a number of newspapers. They, too, can be margined heavily, and there is a futures market. Since they fluctuate with the day-by-day changes in interest rates, they are a good vehicle for making money when the rates fall.

Treasury Bonds

Treasury bonds take over the maturity range where the notes leave off—from 7 years to 30 years. Like the notes, they pay interest semi-annually and their prices are quoted in the daily financial pages. In case you are wondering whether they fluctuate enough to be profitable (or unprofitable), just look at a few of the older issues which were sold back at a time when the Fed was pushing money into the banking system. Some of them, with the low coupon rates that prevailed when they were first issued, have sold for as low as 60 cents on a dollar.

So, the volatility of Treasury bonds can be enough for anyone to make a great deal of money, provided he picks the right direction. What's more, the Treasury can't call the bonds in advance of their maturity, as can some corporate issuers. The idea is to leave the corporations free to take advantage of a rising bond market. They can force the owners of their bonds to sell out just at the time when they are getting ready to really make good. It's a one-way street for some corporations, on which the Treasury can't travel.

Overall, Treasury bonds are probably the best middle-of-the-road choice for cashing in on a decline in interest rates. You don't have to worry about the credit risk, no matter how bad the economy becomes. And they can be bought with very little margin, if you want to be more speculative.

Government Agencies

There are a number of creations of the federal government, such as the Government National Mortgage Association, the Federal Home Loan Banks, the World Bank, the Federal Land Bank and the Farm Credit Bank. They all issue bonds, notes, and bills similar to those of the Treasury. It is widely believed that those issues are direct obligations of the federal government. Actually, they are not; but the government stands behind their performance. So they are the next safest things to Treasuries and they sell only slightly lower.

Perhaps the most interesting of these bonds are those of the Government National Mortgage Association—nicknamed Ginny Mae—because they are different than the rest. Pools of mortgages are assembled by savings and loan companies or other lenders. If they qualify, they can get a Ginny Mae guarantee and are sold to the public at a fixed interest rate. The sponsors of the pools of mortgages collect the payments and send out a *monthly* check which includes both interest and amortization, which can be reinvested, if the owner so desires. For people who need an income that comes in monthly, Ginny Maes are made to order. And, for those who want to speculate, there is a futures market.

Corporate Bonds

There are a huge amount of publicly traded issues ranging from the kingpin, American Telephone, all the way to those of companies that are in bankruptcy. They all pay higher rates than Treasury bonds, so sophisticated buyers can tailor a risk–reward ratio to suit themselves. Much help is provided by such organizations as Standard and Poor's and Moody's, which do a careful job of analyzing and rating the financial conditions of many corporations. It helps to keep investors from having to wade through endless amounts of financial reports.

The corporate bond market will follow the interest movements of Treasuries, and will give you a better return while you are waiting to make your capital gains. But, in our depressed economic environment, a great deal of caution is called for. A number of well-known companies may appear on the sick list before we get through! After all, who would have thought that International Harvester could be going through the mill as it is today? So, if you are going to play the corporate bond market for the decline in interest rates, make sure that the credit of the companies you choose is first rate.

New Wrinkles in Corporate Bonds

With bonds as hard to place as they have been recently, a number of new ways to sell them have been created. One of the most unusual is the zero-coupon bond which pays no interest at all! Instead, like T-bills, they are sold at discounts and the buyer is paid off when the bonds mature. For example, they may be priced at $500 originally, with a payoff of $1000 at maturity. It's an advantage to corporations because, while they may set aside some money for the eventual payment, they have more flexibility in dealing with their flow of cash. One of the problems is that an awfully big payment—known as the "bullet"—comes due immediately on the maturity date. Buyers had better be sure that the corporations make proper provision for that, rather than letting it all pile up at once.

It was once thought that zero-coupon bonds would allow buyers to avoid reporting taxable interest each year; instead, it was hoped that they would be charged at the lower capital gains rate when they were paid off. But the IRS put the freeze on that by requiring an annual amortization. Abroad, where capital gains in some countries aren't taxed at all, zero coupons created quite a stir. The Japanese, especially, were large buyers until their government stopped it. Nonetheless, zero coupons are still traded in quantity.

Still another wrinkle is to issue bonds that pay interest far below prevailing rates, and are sold at a large discount from their maturity price. It's simply another less-exaggerated way of accomplishing much the same thing as zero coupons.

Deep Discount Bonds

Some bonds weren't issued at discounts, but are selling at them because they've been around for a long time. Years ago, interest rates were so much lower than they are today that long-term bonds issued then are selling far below their maturity prices. Take the Pacific Telephone 7¼'s which expire in 2008. Each $1000 bond sold recently for only $500, in keeping with today's yields. However, they have a few advantages.

They aren't apt to be called even if interest rates move sharply lower.

They represent a $1000 claim on the issuing company, so there's a little extra security if the corporation gets into trouble.

So, in a period of rapidly declining interest rates, they often out-perform bonds that are selling close to their maturity prices. It's a good way to invest in the bond market, provided you can be sure that the reason for the low price is related only to the interest rate level, and not to doubts about the health of the company.

Tax Exempt Bonds

States and municipalities are allowed to issue bonds, the interest on which is not subject to federal tax. However, unless they come from an issuer within the state in which the taxpayer lives, they can be subject to state and local taxes—an inducement for investors to buy local issues.

Recently, tax-free bonds have performed even worse than the rest of the market, partly because the scheduled reduction in federal taxes takes away some of their after-tax advantage over taxable bonds. However, there's another reason as well. Revenues in some states and cities have been reduced by the recession, or by the result of taxpayer revolts. Add to that the cutback in federal grants and payments that President Reagan's program calls for, and it's enough to challenge the financial ability of some localities. So, before you buy tax-frees, you'd better check their ratings with some service like Standard and Poor's or Moody's. Your broker can easily get them for you.

Some bond issuers have tried to improve their credit worthiness by insuring their payments with letters of credit from banks that are willing to stand behind their interest and principal requirements—for a fee. A recent issue of Puerto Rican bonds, for example, carried such a letter of credit from a group headed by the Bank of America and the Mellon Bank. A few other issuers provide insurance from such private organizations as AMBAC or the Municipal Bond Insurance Association. Since these props allow the municipalities to pay lower interest rates, they are being used more and more.

There are still other inducements being offered to buyers of hard-to-sell municipals. For instance, New York's Municipal Assistance Corporation (Big MAC) attached a warrant to each $5000 bond entitling its holder to buy a like amount of bonds at the same rate. It's an extra way for bondholders to cash in if interest rates decline.

All of those devices to make tax-frees more palatable are simply the result of the fact that they have been the most depressed area of the bond market. Their yields are nearer to those of Treasuries than they have ever been. For investors, that spells opportunity. In addition, there is an increasing probability that taxes will have to be raised to stop the flow of red ink in the federal budget and to make up for declining state and local revenues. There's a good chance that tax-frees will be among the best performers in the next bull market for bonds.

Speculating in Bonds

When interest rates began to fluctuate sharply, many of the people involved in the market became more interested in price movements than in clipping coupons and collecting interest. Following the example of commodities markets, several exchanges began to allow trading in bond *futures*. Although the first trading started as recently as 1975, by now it is far larger than that of the commodity markets on which they are modeled. Their attraction is that for a very small amount of money, the buyer can get the price appreciation of a large amount of bonds. But, a word of caution! It's a two-way street, in which you can lose as fast as you can make unless you are on the right side of the market.

What is a Future?

Interest rate futures are contracts to either deliver or to take delivery of a specified amount of a financial instrument (Treasury bonds, notes or bills, for example) at a date sometime in the future and at a price established when you buy or sell the contract. There is usually a pretty broad choice of dates, falling due every three months (March, June, September, and December) for 3 or 4 years into the future. You pay more the further out in the future you go, but the broad movements of the market are almost always in the same direction.

Not every brokerage firm will handle orders from individual investors, but there are plenty that will. Most of them establish their own margin demands somewhere above the minimum requirements, but always very low compared to the amount of bonds you control.

While the futures contract implies that you will deliver or take delivery of the bonds, that hardly ever happens. More than 90% of all interest rate futures are sold out (or covered, if they are short sales) well before the delivery date and the participants pocket their profits or pony up their losses.

One of the reasons for the huge size of the futures markets is that institutions, banks, and insurance companies use them for hedging purposes. For example, savings banks know that their businesses will improve if interest rates go down, so they may decide to protect themselves just in case they go up instead. They can do that by selling futures contracts short. That way, if interest rates do go down, they'll lose some money on their short sales, but they'll more than make up for it in operating profits. On the other hand, if rates go up, they will have the consolation of making at least some profits in the market. There are a number of very active futures markets.

T-Bills

Each T-Bill contract is for $1 million worth of them! But you don't have to be rich to buy them. The minimum margin requirement is $2000, although most brokers will demand more. And you should be willing to put up more to avoid continual margin calls if the market goes even slightly against you. After all, a 1-point move in interest rates will mean a difference of $10,000 per contract, five times the minimum margin.

T-Bill futures are traded on the International Monetary Market, a division of the Chicago Mercantile Exchange.

T-Bond Futures

When you buy one contract, it's for $100,000 worth of 8% Treasury bonds. That doesn't mean that you will ever take delivery of 8% bonds. It simply indicates that the prices of the futures are pegged against the value that an 8% bond *would* have in the present market. So, if the market for the latest issue of long-term Treasury sells to yield 13.4%, the nearest month of T-bonds would sell for about 62½ ($62,500 for the $100,000 contract). The minimum margin requirement is $2250—a tiny amount compared to the $100,000 worth of bonds you've contracted for. But, remember that a fluctuation of one point results in a profit or loss of $1000, and there have been times when the futures have gone up or down by as much as 4 or 5 points in a couple of weeks. Clearly, you can make a great deal, if you are right. But, it's a good idea to be prepared with more than the minimum margin.

Treasury-bond futures trade on the Chicago Board of Trade.

Other Interest-Rate Futures

The Chicago Board of Trade allows dealings in Ginny Mae futures—in units of $100,000 pegged to a coupon level of 8%; and in 90-day domestic certificates of deposit. The International Monetary Market allows trading in Bank Certificates of Deposit, in units of $1 million; and in 3-month Eurodollar Time Deposit futures. They all have one thing in common. You get a big bang for the buck!

Interest Rate Options

The newest thing in the bond market is options. Soon, all of the debt securities on which futures are traded will also have options markets. The important difference is that when you buy options you pay a premium for them, and that's all you can ever lose. Once you've paid the initial amount it costs to own them, you won't have to put up any more money, even if the market does go against you. You can ride out any temporary setbacks and still make a great deal of money when interest rates eventually come down. With futures, on the other hand, you may have to pony up more margin during those setbacks—and in a fast moving market that can get discouraging.

An option will cost more than the minimum margin requirement for futures. But, the fact that you can never lose more than your initial investment will allow you to plan your risk—and to be around to cash in on the sharp decline in interest rates that is coming.

Conclusion

There are many ways to take advantage of the bond market's potential rise. Since the markets are quite complicated, the first requirement is to find a good broker whose firm trades in futures, interest-rate options, and in the bonds themselves. Make sure that he knows what he is doing, and that his firm has chartists who keep track of short-term fluctuations. That can help you avoid many of the pitfalls that can happen along the way.

Once you've got a good broker working for you, start slowly so that you can get more confident. After that, you can begin to increase the size of your positions.

Remember that the first money to be made in disinflation will be in the bond market. After that, be prepared to take your profits and throw them into the stock market. That's a one-two punch which will let you get richer once our economy becomes accustomed to disinflation and begins to make its way back to a position from which it can begin to expand once again.

CHAPTER 7

Making Money in the Stock Market

On one of those dreary days of 1974, as the stock market was grinding toward its low, I had lunch at the Stock Exchange Luncheon Club with an investment adviser whom I respect and admire. The gloom at the Club was thick enough to cut with a knife, and the conversation at our table was no exception. Naturally enough, we talked about the market from start to finish. Both of us were troubled by the way in which even stocks with great intrinsic value had taken a nose dive along with the rest. Toward the end of lunch, I illustrated the point by telling of a company that I followed pretty closely. It was selling at an incredibly low level of only 2½ times my estimate of the coming year's earnings. My dining companion topped me with a company that was selling at only 1½ times the cash flow that it would generate in 1974. We both nodded sadly, finished our coffee, and went back to our offices. It wasn't until I thought about our conversation about an hour later that the unusual part of it began to occur to me. I figured that we could get a pretty good laugh out of it, so I called my luncheon companion and pointed out that we had both talked about stocks that were selling at bargain levels, but that things were so bad that neither of us had bothered to ask the other the names of the companies.

That should have been a tip-off that the time to buy was close at hand. In fact, we both sensed that, but we were so busy licking our wounds that we were slow to take advantage of it. It's a truism of Wall Street that when a couple of professionals aren't interested in hearing about new opportunities, it's time for a change of direction of the market. You'll hear much about market timing techniques that claim infallibility, but the best one that I know is this: When you would be suspicious if someone offered to sell you a dollar for only 50 cents, start planning your buying program, and begin to execute it. The reverse is also true. When you listen with rapt attention to your neighbor's latest tips on the market, and when stockbrokers are the most popular people at cocktail parties, stop listening. It's time to start getting out.

In fact, our indication from that lunch at the Stock Exchange turned out to be right on the money. I still don't know the name of the other stock, but the one that I had in mind made good in a big way. What's more, it wasn't at all exceptional. A huge number of stocks doubled and tripled within the next two years. Perhaps the big companies, such as those that make up the Dow Jones Industrial Average, weren't such spectacular performers. But medium-sized and smaller companies had a field day.

To see just how well they did, let's take a sampling from the American Stock Exchange. There were so many outstanding performers that listing them would take pages. So, I've confined the list to 35 stocks, in a variety of industries, all of the names of which began with the letter "A." I've compared their lows in 1974 with their highs in 1976 and 1980. Perhaps that's unfair. You would have to have rabbit's feet *and* horseshoes to buy at the low and sell at the high. But, you wouldn't have *had* to! Some of the advances were among the best in Wall Street's history. And there were so many of them that you would have plenty of opportunity and time to take advantage of them:

Company	Low—1974	High—1976	High—1980
Acme United	1⅞	4½	22⅜
Adams Resources	1½	3⅛	26¾
Adams Russell	¼	2½	28
Adobe Oil and Gas	2⅜	7⅝	46⅞
Aero-Flow Dynamics	2	9½	39¼
Aeronca	2	9½	39¼
Affiliated Capital	1	3⅞	10⅞
Affiliate Hospital Products	2¾	9½	6
Affiliated Publications	3¾	7¼	32½
After Six	1¾	8¼	6¼
Air Express International	⅛	3	24⅝
Almy Stores	1½	6	9½
Alpha Industries	½	1½	30¼
Altamil Inc.	1⅛	6½	16⅜
Alterman Foods	6	14¼	19⅞
American Controlles Ind.	5¾	7½	21⅝
American Maize Products	3⅞	15⅛	20⅞
American Medical Buildings	1¼	3⅞	8¼
American Motor Inns	⅞	3⅜	21⅞
American Petrofina	24¾	34	71
American Precision	1⅛	5	9⅛
American Science and Engineering	1	13⅞	12½
American Seating	3	12¼	16⅝
Anderson Jackson	1¼	3⅝	25½
Anglo Energy	1⅜	2⅞	36⅞
Applied Data Research	1	5⅜	25¼
Argo Petroleum	2¾	4¾	25⅞
Armatron International	1	9⅞	5
Asamera Inc.	5¼	16¼	27⅝
Astrex Inc.	5¼	16¼	27⅝
Atlas Consolidated Mining	1	3¾	9½
Audiotronics	1	4½	12
Automatic Switch	5¼	11	33½
Avemco Corp.	1⅜	4	13⅛

If you had bought most of these stocks, even well above the 1974 lows, you would have had a very nice profit by 1976. Not all of them kept going until 1980, which means that you can't just put *any* stock away and ignore it. But, if you'd re-examined them after the first handsome gains, and decided to hold on to them, most would have made you incredibly large profits by 1980. So large, in fact that it may seem as though it was a once-in-a-lifetime opportunity. Don't you believe it! A similiar opportunity should come again after the United States has become used to operating in a disinflationary economic environment.

Of course, it's not easy to be a buyer when the market is near its bottom. It may not be too difficult to tell that the *time* is right. But you must have the cash available to go to work with. It's pointless to choose sensational values if you are more or less fully invested and you've got to spend your energy in keeping your fingers crossed for a good enough recovery to make up your losses. The first step in successful investing is to be prepared for the opportunities by having sold out before the market really slides. That always takes courage, and even most of the people who make their livings in Wall Street don't often have it. But there has seldom been so obvious a set of signs of trouble ahead as there is right now. Anyone who doesn't get into a liquid position is just ignoring the signals or is being swept away in the general euphoria of hopes for the Reagan administration. It's dangerous to play that game. The first thing to do about your investment program is to sell some of your assets and to put the money into a safe place such as short-term Treasuries or into the bond market, if you want to take advantage of the first profit opportunity. The idea is not to listen to the prophets of doom who would have you run away and put your money into bags of silver and a year's worth of groceries. It's much more likely that the economic recession we are seeing will not turn out to be a catastrophe, but that instead, it will benefit those who have prepared for it when it uncovers some pretty spectacular ways to make money. After all, the history of the United States is that the plums fall to those who are ready and able to invest when everybody else is just trying to recover from their mistakes. *So, get yourself into a position to buy later on.*

How to Phase in Your Investments

Having a program is the key to successful investment. Even if you haven't a large amount of money now, you should take your finances as seriously as though you had a million dollars. One reason for a program is that you (like almost all professionals in Wall Street) are unlikely to sell at the top or to buy at the low, in spite of the advertisements in the financial press which indicates that there are experts who will gladly sell you services which can ring a bell within days of the top or the bottom. Don't put too much faith in them! Generally, they have had their share of successes and many of them work very hard at their techniques. But no one has been infallible for very long. A far more sensible approach is to assume that the market will continue to go down after you have begun to buy. That's why it's necessary to have a program rather than to close your eyes and plunge in. Pick out a list of stocks that you'd like to own, complete with the prices at which you would like to own them. Then as the market drives down to the prices that you've set, start to buy. *Do* think of yourself as a large investor. After all, your money is important enough for you to take just as much care as a large investor.

One of the smartest operators that I've known used to start out by buying one-quarter of the amount of stock that he eventually wanted. If the market went any lower, he'd buy another quarter, and so on until he had his total position at prices that sometimes surprised him. Of course, if the stock went up, he might not buy the rest of his position—except, perhaps, by paying more if the situation showed significant improvement. But, in any event, he had a profit, and a comfortable position for watching for the next opportunity.

Once you've decided on your overall strategy and your sense of timing, you still have a way to go. Now, you have to relate your strategy to individual stocks. No one, after all, can buy the market in general. It's individual issues that you will wind up with. What you are looking for is a group of stocks in which the downside risk is relatively small compared to the upside potential. It really isn't as difficult an assignment as it sounds.

How to Go About Picking Stocks

The first and most important step in a stock selection program is to accept the fact that it is a do-it-yourself job. Naturally, there are good, well-informed brokers available, and many of them are backed by excellent research departments. And both the broker and the research department will be necessary to get you the information you need. So start out by choosing your broker, or even several of them. Make sure that if there are more than one, they have different viewpoints about both the market and about the kinds of stocks they favor. Understandably enough, most research departments spend much of their energy on stocks that are in current vogue and chances are that those aren't the ones that should interest you and almost certainly only a few will be the big winners over a long period of time. The stocks that will make good are more likely to be those that are sufficiently forgotten about to be selling at extraordinary values. To unearth them, *you* are going to have to ask the right questions.If you do, most brokerage firms can give you the answers you need.

Naturally, it's going to take time. But why shouldn't it? In most cases, the ability to produce a good investment program will help you to accumulate more cash than you can get together in any other way. So, it's as important to give it the time that it needs as it is to work at your job. In most cases, you'll have to set aside three or four hours a week to do a good job. You'll have to give at least a glance at the financial press, such as the *Wall Street Journal, Barron's, Business Week,* and *Forbes* because they will not only keep you well-informed, but they will give you some ideas about individual stocks to study. Then, you'll have to ask your broker to have his research department send you its reports and to provide you with the other information that you need. Don't be afraid to tackle the job. It is really much simpler than it sounds and it is likely to be more rewarding than most other things that you are doing about your finances. Chances are that after a remarkably short period of time, you will become quite expert, especially if you start out by using some tried and true techniques.

Techniques to Use

The "Neighborhood Store" Approach

This approach is not suitable for the very large, far-flung multinational giant corporations. They are extremely difficult to analyze. That's why Wall Street has become so accustomed to throwing up its hands and simply looking at the per share earnings reports. But there is absolutely no reason to carry that kind of thinking over to the medium-sized companies, which are likely to be the most interesting investments. Don't be snowed by the so-called experts who try to convince you that the job is so complicated that only they hold the key to success. According to many of them, you have no choice but to rely on their expertise. It's not true. In fact, the key to most medium-sized companies is simply to think of them as a grown-up version of your friendly grocery store. Using what I call the "neighborhood store" technique, you can unlock most of what you will want to know with relative ease.

Suppose the owner of the neighborhood grocery store wanted to retire to Florida and asked you to put together a group of friends to buy him out, promising to make you an offer that would be impossible to resist. If you felt that there was some real money to be made, you'd be glad to give a few nights and weekends to the job. So, you'd begin to analyze just what the store was really worth. *You would use exactly the same methods that you would in analyzing the value of stocks that are publicly traded.*

Chances are that the first thing you'd like to know would be how much cash it could get its hands on right away. Naturally, you'd look at the bankbook to see how much was on deposit. Perhaps, if the business had done well, it would also have some extra money invested in some high-yielding bonds. Then, of course, there would be the inventory. That could prove to be a little more complicated because the goods on hand would have to be sold before they could be turned into actual cash. You'd be anxious to know just how difficult that would be. One way to get a general idea would be to take a look at the daily sales volume and calculate how many days it would take to sell out. Perhaps you'd have to offer some sort of a price discount if you wanted to sell it all out quickly. It's important to be careful because if the business is at all typical, inventories represent the largest share of the items that can be readily turned into cash. Finally, if the store sold on credit, it would have money due from its clients. If the neighborhood is fairly prosperous, chances are quite good that you can collect most of those bills in fairly short order. Total the bank account, the receivibles, the investments and the inventory, and you have the assets that can be turned into cash without too much difficulty. It's exactly the same even for a much larger company. These items are known as "Current Assets" in the balance sheet of the firm, indicating that their value can be realized in a reasonable amount of time. Strangely enough, it's actually much easier to figure what these assets are in the average publicly traded company because the figures have all been analyzed by a certified public accountant. In the case of the grocery store, you'd have to spend the time to dig out the figures yourself.

Once you've pulled together the rough estimate of the amount of cash the grocery store had on hand, the next thing to do is to subtract its debts. First, there's the amount you must pay to those who had supplied merchandise and foods. Added to that would be amounts due to the workers, plus taxes that have already accrued. If the store had any short-term bank loans coming due, you'd have to deduct them as well. Rent owed for the store would also have to be figured into the total short-term debt. So, you'd add up the total of all of these amounts, which are commonly called "current liabilities" and subtract it from the estimate of the cash you could realize in the business. The resultant sum would be the net current assets of the grocery store. Naturally, if you could buy the store for less than that amount, it would be a wonderful deal because it would not take into consideration anything at all for the value of the store as a going business or for its future earning power.

The rest of your analysis would be somewhat more complicated. You'd have to take the non-current assets into consideration. They would include the furniture and fixtures, perhaps including some delivery trucks. Chances that you would want to put those items into the pot only after you had taken a fairly good-sized discount from the amount that the original owner had paid for them even after whatever depreciation he had taken. Against that you'd want to deduct any mortgages or other fixed debt he had to incur in order to buy them. If you added the net amount of these figures to the net current assets, you'd have the total value that you might realize if you were to sell the business. It's a different value than that which is carried on the books because of the estimated discounts to be taken to allow you to liquidate the business in a hurry. *Now*, you'd be ready to deal with the owner of the store. If he is willing to sell for substantially less than the liquidating figure, chances are that you can pick up a good sum quickly by buying it.

Using the Same Method for Picking Stocks

When you have finished the job on the grocery store, you have done a "balance sheet analysis." Maybe it seems unreasonable to think that some of the large companies with a very good on-going business can be bought on the same basis as the corner grocery store. But they can! In fact, it is much more likely that you will be able to find undervaluation among listed securities than in your neighborhood stores. The reason is that Wall Street concentrates so hard on earnings and dividends that the analysis of the balance sheets is almost forgotten. In a prosperous economy it is reasonable to think that any good company can put together a pretty satisfactory earnings record. But, in a recession the tune changes. A number of companies are likely to find it impossible to keep their

profits on the rise. Their stocks are likely to decline in a bear
market to the point where you'd grab the entire company at
the price, if you could. That's the time that balance-sheet
analysis really pays off. This is what the Balance Sheet of a
typical listed corporation looks like:

Consolidated Balance Sheet

ASSETS	LIABILITIES
Current Assets	*Current Liabilities*
Cash and short-term deposits	Bank loans payable
Accounts receivable	Accounts payable
Inventories (lower of cost	Income tax payable
or market)	Accrued Employer Compensation
Prepaid expenses	Dividends payable
Short-term investments	Long-term debt due within year
Total current assets	*Total current liabilities*
Long-term investments	Long-term debt
Fixed assets	Deferred taxes
Deferred contract costs	Preferred stock
	Common stock
	Earned surplus
	Capital surplus
Total assets	Stockholders equity
	Total Liabilities

It may look a bit more formidable than that of the grocery store, but it's really just a little more expanded. Go
about your analysis in just the same way. Total the current
assets which are neatly listed together in every companies
annual and quarterly reports. Subtract the current liabilities, and divide by the number of shares outstanding. If the
stock is selling for near the per-share value of the net
current assets, you've got enough *prima facie* evidence to
warrant a further look at the fixed assets versus the long-
term debt and any other items such as preferred stock or
convertible bonds that may take a chunk of value away
from the common stock. In the kind of depressed stock

market that is likely during the forthcoming recession, you should find enough candidates for buying at substantial discounts to make you more than anxious to put your money to work.

Just to give you an idea of how this kind of analysis works, here are a few examples.

Benjamin Graham was a past master at balance sheet analysis and he made a fortune for himself and his followers. Fortunately for those of us who came after him, he was generous enough to lecture and write about how he did it.

You can get an idea of how Graham used balance sheet analysis to pinpoint stocks that were selling at a bargain from the following table published in a book entitled *The Intelligent Investor*.

The interesting aspect of this table is in the difference between the figures I have called "Line 1", the market price of the stocks, and "Line 2", the net current assets behind each share. You'll notice that in all cases, the net current assets ranged from 1.6 to over 2 times the selling price of the shares. Also, in each case, the net tangible assets on "Line 3", which included the plant and property, was more than double the selling price. The earnings had to be included in the analysis just to be sure that they weren't falling apart in a way that could eat into the assets. Since each of the companies was earning money, there wasn't much to worry about from that score.

Don't be surprised that the amount of shares outstanding in each of these companies was so small. That was the fashion then; by now, after the long economic expansion since the 1950s most companies have split their shares many times. That doesn't change this type of analysis. However, it is true that balance sheet analyses are far easier to make for medium-sized companies than for giants and the difference between the value of the assets and the selling price of the stock is more likely to be made up either by a take-over or some other means which favor the stockholders. I was lucky enough to follow the Graham principles, and be an owner of a few shares of Marshall Wells and Foster Wheeler. They proved to be very profitable investments.

Six Common Stocks Undervalued in 1949

	Cleveland Worsted	Foster Wheeler	Grinnell Corporation	Harnischfeger	Marshall Wells	Saco-Lowell
Average price of common 1949 (Line 1)	67	26³/₈	27¹/₄	22	164	29³/₄
Number of shares	137,300	285,000	500,000	285,000	57,000	300,000
Average market value of common issue	$ 9,200,000	$ 7,518,000	$13,625,000	$ 6,270,000	$ 9,348,000	$ 8,925,000
Senior securities (at call price)	. . . .	2,090,000	. . . .	1,575,000	2,415,000	. . . .
Average market value of capital funds	$ 9,200,000	$ 9,608,000	$13,625,000	$ 7,845,000	$11,763,000	$ 8,925,000
Net assets for capital funds Dec. 1949	$20,900,000	$21,614,000	$35,085,000	$19,542,000	$27,282,000	$21,190,000
Per share of common stock:						
Net current assets (less senior issues) (Line 2)	$125.75	$45.50	$44.62*	$38.80	$345	$46.80
Net tangible assets (book value) (Line 3)	152.87	68.70	70.17	63	437	70.63
Earned 1947	33	3.33	10.78	10.46	69.60	10.06
Earned 1948	39.19	11.95	14.50	11.94	69.30	13.67
Earned 1949	19.08	13.24	12.51	6.50	36.15	16.32
Total 3 years 1947–1949	$ 91.27	$28.52	$37.79	$28.90	$175.05	$40.05

*Includes estimated working capital of Canadian subsidiary.

Sometimes you have to look at the accountant's footnotes to the financial statements. That was true of another of the companies that Graham analyzed—American Hawaiian Steamship. The company had claims against the Government and increased value in some securities it owned that weren't shown in the balance sheet, but did appear in the footnotes. Adding those figures in, Graham was able to come up with a value of $77 a share, mostly in liquid assets. That was far above the $40 at which the stock was selling.

Balance Sheet Position of American Hawaiian Steamship Company, December 31, 1947

Ordinary Cash		$ 4,506,000
Special Cash Funds		17,503,000
Marketable Securities		4,510,000
Receivables and Inventory		6,739,000
		$33,258,000
Less: Current Liabilities	$6,474,000	
Reserve for Capital Gains Tax	3,820,000	
		10,294,000
Net Liquid Assets, as Reported		$22,964,000
Add: Claims and Current Values not stated	est. $8,000,000	
Less Taxes Thereagainst	est. 2,500,000	5,500,000
Total Liquid Assets for Capital Stock		$28,464,000
Fixed Assets		813,000
Prepaid Accounts		1,287,000
Total Assets for Capital Stock		$30,564,000
Per Share on 396,000 Shares		$77

It took some years for the maximum profit to be realized in American Hawaiian, but like in so many situations of this type, the undervaluation prompted a number of changes. There was a transfer of control, and reacquisition of a large part of the stock by the company. At one point, years later, the stock sold at $140, well over triple the $40 selling price at the time of the Graham analysis.

Balance sheet analysis is an art that is being widely practiced today. It is responsible for a number of take-overs, re-purchase plans, and spin-offs that make the head-lines in the financial pages. And there will be more of it in weak recession-oriented market, as stock prices fall. The good thing about it is that it gives one a feeling of safety to know that the assets of a company are worth more than you are paying for the stock, and that some day that value is apt to be realized. It's a more secure yardstick than price–earnings multiples at a time when profits, in general, are likely to decline.

The Parts are Worth More Than the Whole

In elementary arithmetic the whole is equal to the sum of the parts. But not in the stock market. Just look at Esmark, which was the subject of one of the more interesting deals of 1980 and one of the most profitable for its stockholders. Esmark was called Swift and Co., but it changed its name so that it could lose its identification with the meat-packing industry which was held in such low regard by the invest-ing public. After all, management felt, it had diversified into fertilizers and specialty chemicals (its Estech divi-sion), underwear and personal products (Playtex), automo-tive products, and above all, into energy (through its Vickers division). But, all efforts to change its image fell on deaf ears. The stock sold at under $30 a share in spite of earnings of over $4, ignoring the fact that at that price, the Vickers division alone was worth almost as much as the whole company. Then, along came Mobil Oil, which wanted to get control of the Vickers assets. It used a rather new device, intended to save taxes for Esmark. Instead of simply buying the assets for cash, Mobil offered $60 for nearly 12 million shares of Esmark, over double the amount that the stock had fetched before word of disposal of Vickers was made known. It then traded in the Esmark shares it had bought for the Vickers assets and Esmark retired the stock. That, of course, increased the new per-share earnings, which could now be figured on a smaller amount of outstanding shares. It was a wonderful deal for both Mobil and the shareholders of Esmark. It pushed Wall Street research departments into a search for other companies that could show a similiar picture. There are many of them, especially in cases where natural resources divisions are stirred up together in a corporate pot that has a number of industrial segments.

How did this crazy Wall Street mathematics come into being? It is all due to the fact that the market tends to look at earnings rather than underlying values. That knife cuts both ways, of course. It leads to a number of the so-called glamor stocks selling at prices which can't be justified by any possible consideration of the value of the assets. During the 1960s when stock buyers simply exuded optimism, clever deal-makers were taking advantage of that optimism by simply creating glamor. It was all done by mirrors with a kind of now-you-see-it, now-you-don't magician's trick. The technique worked like this. Take a few companies in a dull business, such as metal fabrication or the making of auto parts, but make sure that they have good earnings. Since they are in unglamourous fields, they can be bought comparatively cheaply. Then merge them into a company with plenty of glamor, even though the profits may not be anything to write home about. Finally, change the name of the company to reflect the Marilyn Monroe aspects rather than the Plain Janes which may be making most of the money. During the hey-day of the market of the late 1960s, it was an almost guaranteed way to push the stock to the very high levels that were awarded to glamor companies. All that was needed was a good publicity department to get the earning from the unglamorous divisions lumped in with the glamorous ones to create high appraisal. With the stock selling far above its underlying worth, it could be dealt off to make even more acquisitions.

This led to a new name, the "Conglomerate," and to a group of stocks which gave the 1966-8 bull market a good deal of its sparkle. It looked as though the process could go on forever. All that needed to happen was a regular stream of acquisitions to insure growth, and that could easily be done with a combination of debt, common stock, and such other instruments as warrants. With all of those tricks, a continually higher stream of earnings could be virtually insured. But as we have so often learned in Wall Street, nothing goes on forever. A combination of difficulties hit the conglomerators. First, the trend became so exaggerated that some rather minor companies started to make passes at some of those that were rather large and well-entrenched. Corporate managements with political influence and no desire to be bought out began to fight back, persuading State Securities Commission to aid them. Finally, a medium-sized insurance company tried to get control of the Chemical Bank, and that was enough to get the Congress itself involved.

As if those new political obstacles weren't enough, Richard Nixon became President and decided to fight inflation with a combination of higher interest rates and price controls. The conglomerators, no longer able to afford to use debt to push ahead, began to run into difficulties in meeting the payments on some of the enormous loans that they had built up. They were forced to pause for breath. That was all that was needed to end the magic trick. Conglomerates went out of fashion and by the mid-1970s they were demoted from the darlings of the market to one of its most depressed groups. In fact, many of them had to slim down by disposing of a number of their divisions so that they could keep their heads above water. Once the ability to pile up more debt for more acquisitions was over, there was no way for any but the strongest to keep the pot boiling.

However, the conglomerates *did* make a lasting impact on American corporate life. The idea of diversification was brought home to a number of companies which had no particular desire to obtain a glamor rating for their stocks, but only to offer some protection against a slowdown in their major businesses. So, most large companies began to get into the acquisition act. That trend has continued until by this time it is sometimes difficult to tell just where the earnings of a number of companies come from because it is so often from fields quite different from those for which they became famous. U.S. Steel, for example, now derives the lion's share of its profits from its Marathon Oil and its chemical divisions, while the steel making divisions have become weak sisters. Even the major oil companies have expanded into petrochemicals, and Exxon is making a major effort to enter the office equipment business. Some of the diversification efforts have been pretty dismal. Mobil's buy-out of Montgomery Ward proved to produce nothing but a loss leader for that otherwise highly successful oil giant. But the difference between conglomeration and the diversification of the major companies is that the giants can afford to sit through bad times and patiently (although discontentedly) wait for things to straighten out in their own good time. So, a good look at American industry today shows a huge variety of companies, both large and small, with stables of widely varied divisions in areas that are often surprisingly unrelated to the main business of the parent company.

Still, Wall Street pays little attention to this diversification until it must. It continues to walk its usual beat of looking at per share earnings rather than underlying assets. And, in the process, it makes some grave underestimations. Of course, it has a point in some cases. Much of the time nothing will happen to give the stockholders any share of the appreciation in underlying values. Company executives like to hold onto their power and perquisites and they are persuaded to do so by the fact that even if some of the main segments of the business are doing poorly, a few profitable divisions can make it look as though they are doing a good job. So, all too often, the stockholders are relegated to simply picking up their dividends and looking at the net overall earnings that come their way. It is usually only those companies in which the management has large ownership that attempt to do something with the hidden values in the more glamorous segments. Other companies resist offers even though they are far above the stock's selling price, as though the offerers were trying to give them measles rather than making a good offer to the stockholders. As a result, only a handful of the offers that would have substantially benefitted the shareholders have ever trickled through to them, let alone actually come to fruition. In all too many cases managements have protected themselves rather than giving the stockholder a crack at a good-sized profit. Unfortunately, they've even had the protection of the local securities authorities and the laws which were set up to protect the stockholder from being hurt. Those very same laws are frequently used to keep the very people they were trying to protect from reaping substantial benefits.

Still, it's worth keeping track of those companies whose parts are quite valuable because in the difficult times that lie ahead stocks may decline to a point where the shareholders will be very unhappy. If so, it will be difficult for managements which are showing a poor record to resist the attempts of larger companies to pay higher for all of the stock, or at least some of the divisions. That is one of the great opportunities that a poor economic condition can produce for those who have the foresight to buy the stock at depressed prices.

Investing For Growth

There's no question about where the biggest investment gains have originated. There's nothing like putting your money into true growth companies before the rest of the world is aware of them and waiting patiently for them to make good. A few years ago, a fellow Wall Streeter came to see me, hoping that I could give him some ideas about how to use put and call options (see chapter 8) to solve some of his tax problems. His main concern was one that we'd all like to have. Soon after World War I his mother and uncle had a summer house in the country. A neighbor persuaded them to cash in the Liberty Bonds in which they had patriotically invested a few thousand dollars and to buy some of the shares in his newly started company. They did and it made them rich. Their neighbor was none other than Thomas J. Watson, the founder of IBM. By the 1970s, when both mother and uncle had died, their heirs inherited IBM stock worth many millions even after they had each given substantial gifts to their pet charities. It was difficult to give much advice. Selling some calls on IBM stock could improve the return from some of the holdings and under certain conditions it could scale up the prices for the amount of stock that my friend wanted to sell. But it was all fairly limited compared to the enormity of the profit in which he had become heir. I found myself wishing that my father had only decided to own a summer house near Mr. Watson's, instead of speculating in Florida real estate.

There are a few such stories of those Babe Ruths and Lou Gehrigs of the stock market. But, remember that for every clean-up hitter, there are hundreds of also-rans in the big leagues, to say nothing of all of those promising prospects who end up in the minors. I, for one, never expect to have the luck to get into one of the genuine articles near the beginnings of its enormous growth pattern, or to have the patience to hang with it until it can make me thousands of times my money. But, I do expect to be able to buy growth companies early enough in their growth curve to make some good-sized profits. To do that it really isn't necessary to be in on the ground floor. The important thing is to be able to recognize the growth potential before the rest of the world does; chances are that when Wall Street as a whole puts the stocks in the genuine growth category, you should be getting ready to sell out and go on to the next one. That's one way to take advantage of growth. The other is to buy acknowledged growth stocks when the market is so depressed that it carries them right down to very attractive prices along with the rest of the list.

To judge whether growth stocks are selling at attractive levels, we must get involved in the price–earnings multiple. Except for those conclusions which are based mainly on underlying asset value, most decisions made by both buyers and sellers of stocks are related to price–earnings multiples. Very simply, the p/e multiple is derived by dividing the price of the stock by the latest 12 months earnings (that's how it's done in the newspapers and the Standard and Poor's loose-leaf sheets) or, for the more sophisticated, by the forecasted earnings for the upcoming year. Earnings of most companies have their cyclical ups and downs. But the real volatility in the stock market comes from changes in the price–earnings multiples. Just look at the historical record. In 1949 the price–earnings multiple of the stocks making up the Dow Jones Industrial Average was about 7 times their earnings for the preceeding 12 months. It more than matched that again in 1974, when it was a little over 6. During the 25 years in between, the p/e multiple of the Dow gradually rose until it hit 24 times in 1961 almost 4 times over that of 1949 and, of course, a huge number of points in the market. But, 1961 was the high-water mark and from then on until the 1974 there was a gradual, but steady, descent.

Dow Jones Industrial Average Close			P/E Ratio
1945	March 31	154.41	14.9
	June 30	165.29	15.4
	September 29	181.71	17.0
	December 31	192.91	18.3
1946	March 30	199.75	20.5
	June 28	205.62	20.1
	September 30	172.42	14.9
	December 31	177.20	13.0
1947	March 31	177.20	10.7
	June 30	177.30	9.8
	September 30	177.49	9.5
	December 31	181.16	9.6
1948	March 31	177.20	9.3
	June 30	189.46	9.7
	September 30	178.30	8.5
	December 31	177.30	7.7
1949	March 31	177.10	7.4
	June 30	167.42	7.0
	September 30	182.51	7.4
	December 31	200.13	8.5
1950	March 31	206.05	8.9
	June 30	209.11	8.4
	September 29	226.36	8.3
	December 30	235.41	7.7
1951	March 31	247.94	7.7
	June 29	242.64	7.6
	September 28	271.16	9.3
	December 31	269.23	10.1

Dow Jones Industrial Average Close			P/E Ratio
1952	March 31	269.46	10.7
	June 30	274.35	11.4
	September 30	270.61	11.1
	December 31	291.90	11.8
1953	March 31	279.87	10.9
	June 30	268.26	10.0
	September 30	264.04	9.6
	December 31	280.90	10.3
1954	March 31	303.51	11.2
	June 30	333.53	12.1
	September 30	360.46	13.4
	December 31	404.39	14.4
1955	March 31	409.70	13.8
	June 30	451.38	14.1
	September 30	466.62	13.6
	December 30	488.40	13.7
1956	March 29	511.79	14.2
	June 29	492.78	13.9
	September 28	475.25	14.1
	December 31	499.47	15.0
1957	March 29	474.81	13.8
	June 28	503.29	14.4
	September 30	456.30	12.4
	December 31	435.69	12.1
1958	March 31	446.76	13.7
	June 30	478.18	16.3
	September 30	532.09	19.0
	December 31	583.65	20.9
1959	March 31	601.71	19.4
	June 30	643.60	18.0
	September 30	631.68	17.7
	December 31	679.36	19.8
1960	March 31	610.59	18.2
	June 30	640.62	20.5
	September 30	580.14	18.3
	December 31	615.89	19.1

Dow Jones Industrial Average Close			P/E Ratio
1961	March 30	676.63	22.9
	June 30	683.96	23.4
	September 29	701.21	24.2
	December 29	731.13	22.9
1962	March 30	706.95	20.7
	June 29	561.28	16.2
	September 28	578.98	16.3
	December 31	652.10	17.9
1963	March 29	682.52	18.3
	June 28	706.68	18.3
	September 30	732.79	18.2
	December 31	762.95	18.5
1964	March 31	813.29	19.1
	June 30	831.50	18.7
	September 30	875.37	19.1
	December 31	874.13	18.8
1965	March 31	889.05	18.3
	June 30	868.03	17.1
	September 30	930.58	17.6
	December 31	969.26	18.1
1966	March 31	924.77	16.8
	June 30	870.10	15.5
	September 30	774.22	13.5
	December 30	785.69	13.6
1967	March 31	865.98	15.3
	June 30	860.26	15.8
	September 30	926.66	17.6
	December 29	905.11	16.8
1968	March 29	840.67	15.6
	June 28	897.80	16.1
	September 30	935.79	16.4
	December 31	943.75	16.3
1969	March 28	935.48	15.8
	June 30	873.19	14.7
	September 30	813.09	13.6
	December 31	800.36	14.0

Dow Jones Industrial Average Close			P/E Ratio
1970	March 31	785.57	14.5
	June 30	683.53	12.8
	September 30	760.68	14.7
	December 31	838.92	16.4
1971	March 31	904.37	17.3
	June 30	891.14	16.7
	September 30	887.19	16.6
	December 31	890.20	16.2
1972	March 30	940.70	16.6
	June 30	929.03	15.8
	September 29	953.27	15.3
	December 29	1020.02	15.2
1973	March 30	951.01	13.2
	June 29	891.71	11.5
	September 28	947.10	11.5
	December 31	850.86	9.9
1974	March 29	846.68	9.5
	June 28	802.41	8.6
	September 30	607.87	6.1
	December 31	616.24	6.2
1975	March 31	768.15	8.2
	June 30	878.99	10.5
	September 30	793.88	9.5
	December 31	852.41	11.3
1976	March 31	999.45	12.2
	June 30	1002.78	11.1
	September 30	990.19	10.3
	December 31	1004.65	10.4
1977	March 31	919.13	9.6
	June 30	916.30	9.4
	September 30	847.11	9.4
	December 30	831.17	9.3
1978	March 31	757.36	8.5
	June 30	818.95	9.0
	September 29	865.82	8.5
	December 29	805.01	7.1

Dow Jones Industrial Average Close			P/E Ratio
1979	March 30	862.18	6.9
	June 29	841.98	6.5
	September 28	878.58	6.4
	December 31	838.74	6.7
1980	March 31	785.75	6.5
	June 30	867.92	7.5
	September 30	932.42	8.4
	December 31	963.99	7.9
1981	March 31	1003.87	8.1
	June 30	976.88	7.6
	September 30	849.98	6.9
	December 31	875.00	7.7

*Courtesy of William M. Lefevre.

Nothing could show the importance of price–earnings multiple more than this: for a company large enough to be listed in the Dow Jones Industrials to quadruple earnings in the 12 years between 1949 and 1961 was quite a task. It required management skills, large new plants, and equipment. Tens of thousands of people can be involved in pushing up the earnings of a General Motors, Dupont, or Sears. Most of them have to be doing everything right to allow for a quadrupling of earnings. But, from the point of view of the stock price, the same result is accomplished by simply getting the p/e multiple to quadruple. The difference in the amount of time and effort involved is simply astonishing.

Since price–earnings multiples are of such overriding importance to the stock market, you'd think that most professional Wall Streeters would have a pretty good idea of what makes them tick. But, nothing could be further from the truth. Of course, there have been a number of attempts and some of them have seemed logical enough. For example, there are several quite complicated mathematical work-outs which basically tie the price of a stock to the future dividends to the stockholders. Make an estimate of the future earnings, then take a date after which the company will be mature enough to pay out a good percentage of its earnings in dividends—let's say 40%. From then on the mathematics becomes tedious enough to require a computer because it totals the future stream of dividends and then subtracts a percentage of each year's pay out, depending on how far in the future it will occur. Finally, the adjusted stream of future dividends is multiplied by an amount that takes into consideration the level of the stock market and the money market. The number that results from that is supposed to be the logical value of the stock in today's market. Divide that by the estimated earnings for the current year, and lo and behold! You've got a price-earnings multiple. Does that all sound complicated enough to make you throw up your hands in dismay? It does to me and a number of other Wall Streeters. There's something about it that is so over-intellectualized that it really doesn't seem to reflect the stock market's reality, which is often illogical and always emotionally overheated. These complicated formulas seem to be telling the stock market how it *ought* to think, and no one has been able to do that for very long.

So, until someone comes along with a formula which can take into consideration the illogical and often strange behavior of the market in addition to the way in which it *should* behave (if it were only reasonable), we are all right back to trying to fly by the seat of our pants. At least that has the advantage of the fact that we can change our minds frequently, just as the market itself does.

Obviously, the real concern for most of us is whether the p/e's of the individual stocks we follow put them in a buying range. But before we can decide that, we must look at the price–earnings multiple of the market as a whole. That of the Dow Jones Industrials is a good starting place because it is so frequently calculated and reported upon. Once you have got that as a measuring rod, you can begin to appraise the value of individual stocks relative to the standard, rather than trying for an absolute value, which exists only theoretically, in any event. In 1961, with the Dow's p/e up at a stratospheric 24 multiple, it wasn't at all exceptional to see growth stocks selling at 40-50 times estimated earnings; and there were smaller groups of stocks with super-glamorous potentials that actually fetched 100 or more times the estimated earnings. Most of them collapsed badly during the 1962 market decline, which points up the danger of buying *at all* when the market, in general, is at a very high level. In mid-1982, with the p/e multiple of the Dow down at about 7, such astronomical numbers even for stocks that fire the imagination (such as those in the gene-splitting business) are out of the question. Reasonably mature companies even in such growth fields as computers are available for a fraction of the 1961 or 1968 levels. The demise of the lofty multiple can be blamed on competition from other forms of investment. The most obvious is the bond market. With yields of first-class corporate bonds up at close to 15%, the investor must be very sure of the growth of the companies before he buys stocks at anything but bargain levels.

Interest rates not only make bonds serious competition for the investment dollar, but they are no longer as stable as they were during periods of high multiple markets. They move up and down with great volatility these days since the Government and the Federal Reserve Board have decided that it is legitimate to use them to control the economy. Theoretically, as interest rates go up, the competition for the investment dollar becomes so severe that price-earnings multiples are driven down with a negative effect on the stock market as a whole. But the other side of the coin isn't so bright and shining. Interest rates should come down when the recession really becomes deep, but that isn't necessarily good for the stock market, since a poor business climate threatens the earnings of most corporations. That is likely to have a more negative effect on stock prices than high interest rates. So, we are caught on the horns of a dilemma.

A really credible statement of policy from the Federal Reserve could help because it could pin down one side of the problem. At least, it did back in 1970 when the Stock Exchange's Chairman "Bunny" Lasker went to visit his old friend, President Nixon. Sitting with the President as Mr. Lasker walked in was Arthur Burns, the Chairman of the Federal Reserve Board, which had been driving the market into the ground by crunching credit and driving interest rates up to a level that then seemed sky-high (although we would regard them as merely moderate today). Dr. Burns seldom talked in direct terms, and one of the greatest skills in Wall Street in those days was the ability to cut through his words and to interprete his hints and parables about what the Fed's policy would turn out to be. But, by the time of that meeting, both the President and Chairman Burns had had enough. The stock market was close to a panic level, and the bond market was bad enough to keep a number of companies from being able to complete some necessary and legitimate financing. So, for a change, Dr. Burns gave out with a simple and direct statement. The Federal Reserve would, he said, make enough money available to meet the needs of the business community. When that statement hit the press, it was as though a storm cloud had been lifted. It gave the stock market one of the biggest one day bounces in history. Never mind that it took a few months of retreats and new trials before the market could build up a head of steam for a true and sustained upward move. The Burns statement marked the real end of the 1969–1970 bear market.

Nothing that simple is happening in 1982. True, the Federal Reserve and the economists of the Reagan Administration express the pious hope that as the inflation rate moderates, interest rates will decline. But, if they do, it will be only because we have slid into deep recession. Otherwise, there isn't much doubt that we'll be looking at interest rates that will seem shocking even by today's lofty standards.

So, price-earnings multiples will have to fight either high interest rates or a recession. Don't expect them to go up until there are several factors in combination. Wait until the downward thrust of the economy is nearing its end, and interest rates have been stable for some time at levels substantially lower than today's. By then, the p/e multiple for the Dow should be within hailing distance of the 1949 and 1974 lows. Buying opportunities will be obvious for those who have some money to invest. So be prepared!

How to Use Price-Earnings Multiples

When price-earnings multiples become low enough during this recession, there are three methods in which they can point to opportunities.

The easiest way: Even the non-growth blue chips will make you money if you buy them close to their historic p/e levels. But, you must be reasonably sure that the rapid slide in their recession-dented earnings is near its end. You don't have to wait for the recovery to start. In fact, by that time it would be too late to take advantage of the undervaluation. Just be sure that the steepest part of the decline in earnings is over. For that, you should have plenty of coverage by Wall Street firms because most of them follow the blue chips and come up with a constant stream of earnings estimates. Remember that the best time to buy a blue chip is *after* profits have deteriorated and while the price multiple is still near its bottom level.

The reasons for the comparative ease of using this strategy are: (1) the risks are comparatively low and (2) the amount of easily available information about these companies is unusually great. You won't get rich in these stocks, but you can make a wonderful return on your money.

A little more difficult: Buy stocks that are traditionally considered growth stocks, such as computers, office equipment, high-technology, or biological. Just as in the case of the blue chips, there should be adequate coverage by Wall Street research departments, although it isn't likely to be quite as broad as that for blue chips. But, when it comes to price-earnings multiples, you'll have to be a little more careful. Historically, low p/e's are one method of making a selection, but that may prove to be a bit too rigid. After all, you are looking to make a more substantial profit in these growth stocks than in the blue chips and you should be willing to take greater risks. That is especially true in the case of growth stocks which have gone through the recession without suffering very much. For this kind of stock, you should key into the timing of their recovery from the recession rather than looking for a fixed p/e level. Be prepared to pay anything from 1½ to 2 times the p/e level of the Dow for these stocks. They will probably keep or extend this relationship as the recession ends. Their stocks should start to make good early in the stock market's turnaround.

The hardest (and the most profitable) way: Pick out some emerging growth fields those that have not as yet been recognized by the investing public. Chances are that you'll find that companies in these fields are still moderate in size, and that is an advantage. For one thing, they are probably too small to have attracted very much institutional interest so the stock could be selling at prices that don't reflect their future growth potentials. However, this is the most difficult of all selection techniques because it requires the use of imagination and a good deal of thinking about the future. In addition, the companies in these fields are likely to be lightly covered by Wall Street research departments, so you will have to do more of your own digging than for the other kinds of stocks we have been examining.

Syntex Corporation is an excellent example of how profitable imagination and foresight can be. In 1958, Charles Allen, of the Wall Street firm of Allen and Co., decided that Ogden Corporation, a publicly held company in which he had a major interest, should buy Syntex. At the time, Syntex was a little company, with its major factory in Mexico. It had come into being because of stories about the interesting effects that a root, which grew wild in the southern part of Mexico, had on some of the local people that used it. After some experimentation, it was found that the root could be ground up and treated chemically to form into steroids, from which a wide variety of hormones could be made. That was exciting, because until that discovery, many hormones were made of organs of animals or secretions, and, for some potentially useful ones, the entire world's supply was tiny.

However, Syntex was still a small company, and there weren't many people in Wall Street who were interested in it. Besides, it had some problems which put them off. For one thing, a former executive had broken away and formed competing manufacturing facilities. On top of that, there were anti-trust and other suits against it.

Enter Charles Allen, one of the most creative financiers of his generation! He was able to understand the potential of having a very large supply of steroids that could end up as hormones, even if it meant overlooking the immediate problems. So, Ogden bought Syntex and then decided to distribute it to its own shareholders. As a result of that, there were about 1.28 million shares of stock and the opening price when they began to be traded was 8½—giving Syntex a total equity value of approximately $11 million.

Then, the use of hormones grew dramatically, just as Charles Allen had hoped. Of course, the greatest excitement concerned the oral contraceptive, which was only in an experimental stage when Ogden first bought Syntex.

The results were a stockholder's delight. Five years later, in 1963, the stock was split 3 for 1. By mid-January of 1964 the new shares sold as high as $190 before they began to give ground. The then outstanding 4.5 million shares had risen to a market value of over $800 million, over 70 times the original $11 million. Quite a pay-off for creative thinking and the courage to invest in potential growth!

Very few of us can be Charles Allens, but if you are willing to put in the extra work involved, you'll find that the efforts will pay off. Just look at what happened after the 1974 stock market collapse! The smaller domestic oil and natural gas companies received some attention in the aftermath of the OPEC boycott and price increases. But, they were soon forgotten and lapsed back to their old obscurity. After all, the investing public reasoned, price controls for domestic oil and natural gas were still in force and were going to continue for the foreseeable future. So the stocks stayed on their bottoms for some time. Then, it occurred to the more adventurous stock buyers that domestic oil and natural gas were in such demand that the reserves in the ground would eventually make the stocks much more valuable. It really didn't require any great inside knowledge or even any genius to begin to revise the valuations of the domestic companies upward and to understand that their assets in the ground would eventually determine the sel-

ling price of the stocks rather than their earnings per share.
The rewards for understanding this rather simple logic
were enormous. Stocks of the smaller companies with good-
sized domestic reserves rose 4-10 times within the next few
years.

So take some time out to think about the what will become the most dramatically expanding areas of the economy during the recovery from the recession. You'll receive
a substantial pay-off by uncovering some areas which
haven't as yet occurred to most of Wall Street. One way to
go about looking for them is to anticipate the kinds of
things that the United States will need badly enough to
pour money into even in an environment where, except for
defense, the government is very tight-fisted.

Anticipating the National Needs

Somehow, in almost any economic climate, when the
needs of our society become powerful enough, they produce
a number of ways to make large profits in the stock market.
Let's take a glance at history.

The most dramatic events were wars. There can be many
philosophical debates about how long the Great Depression would have continued if it had not been for World War
II. But there isn't much question about what actually happened. Even before Pearl Harbor, the United States
stepped up its production in order to arm England and their
allies who were still fighting against the Fascists. After the
Japanese attack our industry moved into full production.
Excess profits taxes were imposed, but in spite of them a
number of companies were able to regain their financial
health. The stock market was in no great hurry to recognize
the change, and it was terribly troubled in 1942 when it
seemed likely that Germany might win the war. But, then it
began to recognize the extent of our industrial turnaround.
It was interesting that very large profits were made in
areas that were less obvious than the war production companies. They came from those companies that had been the
most depressed before the war began—for example, the
railroads and the public utilities. These companies saw

transportation and electrical demand pick up very sharply, since they were two of the industries that our war efforts needed most. In the case of the public utilities, many of them were still groaning under the debt that had been placed on them during the 1920s by such tycoons as Samuel Insul. The public utility holding companies carried this to its logical extreme. They were actually built like pyramids, with the operating utility companies forming the base. Control of those operating companies was held by still other corporations, which had piled up even more debt until it reached the ultimate holding company which produced no electricity at all, but held control of a number of companies that did. A very small investment in common stock, but an absolutely colossal super-structure of debt!

All of this fancy financing depended on the earnings of the underlying operating companies, which had to show enough profits to service all of the debt. Naturally, when the depression came, their earnings began to decrease instead of increase. So the entire house of cards collapsed into bankruptcy. The same, to a lesser degree, happened to the railroads, many of which were pushed into the hands of the receivers by the collapse of the economy. Then, along came the war and, as if by magic, the operating companies began to pile up earnings. Suddenly, there was enough cash being generated to make arrangements possible with the bondholders and other creditors. Ultimately, the pyramids were reversed and the operating entities freed from the holding company structures. The profits in the defaulted bonds and even in the common stocks of the utilities and railroad holding companies were literally enormous. During the war, while I was stationed in the Pacific, my father bought me a few shares of Electric Bond and Share. He paid $1 a share for it, and when a year or so later it sold at $3, he felt pretty brilliant and unloaded it. Too bad that he didn't hold onto it because by the early 1950s the shares in the underlying operating companies were distributed to the shareholders of Electric Bond and Share, and they were worth well over $100 a share.

Some of the same wartime benefits were reaped during the Korean War, and to a lesser extent during the early part of the Vietnam War. But it isn't necessary to look only at times of war. Even in peace time, there has always been a push toward satisfying the needs of our society. Take the Sputnik. The Soviet Union blew the Space Age wide open by launching the first Earth-circling satellite back on October 4, 1958, when Dwight Eisenhower was President. At first, the official stance of our Government was that there was nothing dramatically new about the Sputnik. It was just a continuation of the ballistic missile that we and the Soviets had been working on. So, the stock market paid little attention to the new development. In fact, we were in the midst of a recession and the market was quite weak. But, behind the headlines, the United States began to mount a major effort to catch and outmatch the Russians. It not only brought about a big enough industrial push to get us out of the recession, but it marked the dawn of the days of advanced science companies as very profitable entities rather than simply as the recipients of research grants. Texas Instruments, for example, developed from a mere baby into an industrial giant. And many very small companies, which had been operating in lofts with a few people putting together transistors by hand, became large companies. The profits in their stocks were enormous. The spread of advanced technology took some unexpected turns for imaginative investors. For example, there was a big push to increase education in science, and words such as "New Math" began to creep into our vocabulary. Textbook publishers were among the major beneficiaries.

During the Kennedy and Johnson Presidencies our space efforts were well in place, and there were no longer any great surprises in store for investors. But, there was a big push toward adapting advanced science to our manufacturing and service industries. Computers changed their roles from tools that were used mostly in scientific laboratories to business machines that had their place in every sizeable company. New names such as Control Data joined IBM in the ranks of rapid growth stocks. The marvel of instant photography made Poloroid spurt. Xerox started a revolution in office procedures. Electronics became a household word and even though there were the usual ups and downs of the stock market, during the decade of the 1960s, companies in the science fields continued to command glamorous price–earning multiples.

The 1970s were a more complicated period. For the most part, the industrialized nations have been struggling with a constant battle between slowing economic expansion to cope with inflation, and the fear of producing a serious enough recession to undermine their political structures. The main new growth area that was uncovered was in oil and natural gas and the exploration for them. Even that was remarkably slow in developing in spite of the impact of OPEC because there was such a wide variety of price controls to protect the consumer against higher prices. But, the needs of our country were too great to keep the oil and gas companies under a cloud forever. Just as in other periods of post-World War II history, large profits were made by those who had the foresight to buy the stocks in the energy producers.

Where do We go From Here?

With a deep and long recession certain, it is a little too early to pick out any of the more esoteric areas into which our country's needs will push us. In fact, it doesn't make any sense to do any buying right now, so there's plenty of time to do your thinking about the future. But, even now, a few areas of long-term growth are beginning to open up. For one thing, there is the defense area. President Reagan has dramatized it by making it one of the few segments of Government spending which he wants to see increase, rather than decrease. So, even the recession isn't likely to hurt companies which concentrate on defense. But, that has been pretty much recognized by the stock market, at least in so far as the large companies with visible contracts are concerned. Still, those very large programs such as the B-1 bomber and the MX missile have their ups and downs. Any sort of political compromises with the Soviet Union can put them on the back burner again. So, the giants in the industry aren't likely to be the best way to play the increase in defense spending. However, there are a number of smaller companies which concentrate on such things as military electronics and communications. They seem to have an assured growth path ahead of them. For one thing, the military forces of the future will be provided with very sophisticated weaponry, and electronics can make up for large forces of troops that are less sophisticatedly equipped. In addition, a number of the technological advances are actually labor saving. They enable our military personnel to be more efficient and our training to be less time consuming. Try to isolate a few stocks in this area to follow until the time comes to buy them.

Still another area that President Reagan is stressing is that of increased efficiency and productivity throughout our entire economy. In fact, the new tax structure is intended to make it easier for companies to spend the money needed to make them more efficient. If history is any guide, an increase in capital spending will mark time until it sees where the economy is headed and then begin to pick up. That will call for new plant construction and for more expensive machine tools, as well as a great number of new methods of using computers. Look also for great new developments in industrial robots. No, we are not yet in the days of the science fiction films, but company executives must be very attracted by the idea of having some of their processes done by noncomplaining machines rather than by bored workers. Once again, pick out a few likely candidates and watch them while you are waiting to invest.

The last of the obvious areas is that of energy. Not simply drilling for, or finding, oil or natural gas! The present glut of oil won't last forever. So long as the industrialized world is dependent on oil, it will be in the not-too-tender mercies of OPEC and the Arab world. That must stop! But it isn't likely to come to an end just because of further exploration for hydrocarbons since there probably isn't enough in the ground in this country to cause a good-sized increase in our reserves after the amounts that we deplete. But, before you become too gloomy about the prospect of getting free of what looks like permanent Arab domination, remember that the United States has been very resourceful about the way in which it responds to challenges that can be met by the use of our industrial power. Think of Sputnik and the need to match Germany's threat by building an Atomic bomb during World War II. It's about time that our scientists began to work in earnest on the energy problem. It may seem as though a long time has passed, but the real drive (and money) needed to push forward alternatives to hydrocarbons hasn't been around for much over 8 years. Already, there are hints of possible progress, although much of it is still in the experimental stage. The main avenues of approach at present are: (1) conversion of coal or shale into a burnable and easily transportable hydrocarbon such as gas or methane. (2) Solar energy either through the use of the sun's rays to heat water or some other compound, or through direct conversion of sunlight into energy at an economic price. (3) Secondary and tertiary recovery of the oil and gas already discovered. We have been able to extract only 30-40% of the hydrocarbons we've found. With prices so much higher than they were a few years ago, a number of methods of extracting the balance may become feasible. Traditional work in this area is done through water, steam, or CO_2 injection into the wells. While that does some good, there is a great deal of research money going into some more advanced methods. Obviously, if something very good is discovered, it can be a much easier way to increase our energy reserves than by just drilling. (4) Conservation of our fuel reserves by other means than just doing without. For example, there has been a revival of the concept of using the same fuel to accomplish several purposes. It has a fancy new name of "co-generation," and it can mean such things as driving an electric power turbine with the necessary amount of fuel and then using the steam to heat buildings. Other potential alternatives include the use of more sophisticated electrical equipment both in the home and industry.

It's a large field and a much needed one. It should give any investor plenty of things to investigate. The best approach is to pick out some interesting companies in each area of energy independence *now*. Since it will undoubtedly be one of the best ways to make money over the next decade, a little bit of study should pay off handsomely.

Once you are aware of what is going on in the field, it should be relatively easy for you to jump in with your investment money early in the game after some of the inevitable breakthroughs occur.

Cash Flow Analysis

Suppose you could assemble the Board of Directors of a company that you might be interested in and ask them any questions you'd like. Chances are that what you'd like to know most is what they think about the future. For example, are they confident enough to pour a large amount of money into new plants and equipment? That might indicate that they have some new products to bring to the market, or at least that they feel good about expanding the production lines of their old products. How are they handling their debt? Are they borrowing more for expansion, or simply to roll over their already outstanding debt? Have they raised new money in the equity market to take care of their expansion? Or perhaps they are playing the future close to the vest by paying down their debt and adopting a conservative position.

Naturally, there isn't any way in which you can expect to assemble the Board to answer your questions. But, you can find a number of the answers in the "Cash Flow" report, often called the "Statement of Changes in the Financial position" or "Source of Funds." It is contained in the Annual Report of most listed corporations, and it is a very valuable item even though it is often ignored by those who concentrate only on earnings per share. The important difference between the earnings statement and the cash flow analysis is that the latter includes the depreciation and depletion allowances, which build up a company's cash and ability to expand, as well as deferred income taxes that are important to a large number of companies (and are likely to become more so under President Reagan's tax proposals). The cash flow report also tells you about the expenditures for new plants and equipment, and about how the company is handling its debt.

Perhaps the most interesting of all cash flow statements

are those of the oil companies. Most major oil exploration companies plow back more than their reported earnings each year into new exploration or into other forms of energy. A major part of the reason is that their depletion and depreciation charges against income are greater than those of most industrial companies. Add to that very large deferred taxes. Some oil companies are best thought of as machines for paying out dividends and for developing new reserves. There could be no better expression of faith in the future! It has led a great number of oil analysts to the conclusion that the cash flow of the oil companies is a far better indication of value than the actual earnings per share.

Standard Oil of California and Subsidiaries
Consolidated Statement of Changes in Financial Planning

	1980	1979*	1978*
Sources of Funds			
Net income	$2,401†	$1,785	$1,089
Depreciation, depletion and amortization	767	707	591
Deferred income taxes	550	257	132
Distributions exceeding equity in current earnings of affiliated companies	254	36	(36)
Funds provided by operations	3,972	2,785	1,776
Increases in long-term debt	41	27	28
Net book value of properties, plant and equipment sold or retired	93	151	59
Increase (decrease) in other non-current obligations	185	(19)	(7)
	4,291	2,944	1,856
Uses of Funds			
Additions to properties, plant and equipment	2,331	1,459	993

	1980	1979*	1978*
Cash dividends	615	495	435
Reductions in long-term debt	214	74	264
Net increase in investments and advances to affiliated companies	133	66	5
Increase (decrease) in deferred charges	92	5	(5)
Other—net	28	28	13
	3,413	2,127	1,705
Increase in Working Capital	$ 878	$ 817	$ 151
Analysis of Changes in Working Capital Increase (decrease) in current assets			
Cash and marketable securities	$1,298	$ (69)	$ 536
Receivables	79	967	614
Inventories	593	243	(222)
Prepaid taxes and other expenses	14	69	56
	1,984	1,210	984
(Increase) decrease in current liabilities			
Accounts and notes payable	(525)	(327)	(397)
Current maturities of long-term debt	(150)	217	(208)
Federal and other taxes on income	(304)	(232)	(207)
Other	(127)	(51)	(21)
	(1,106)	(393)	(833)
Increase in Working Capital	$ 878	$ 817	$ 151

*Restated and reclassified
†Dollars in millions.

A dramatic example of just how different cash flow can be from the reported earnings came in Forest Oil Company's annual report for 1980. Forest is a medium-sized oil and gas company which has attracted attention from analysts because of its relatively large reserves compared to the selling price of the stock. During 1980, its revenues rose to $89 million from $70 million the year before, a satisfactory 27% increase. But it took some noncash write-offs of $5.2 million for some Canadian properties, and it charged off a huge depreciation and depletion allowance of almost $37 million. As a result, net earnings after a small tax payment were a mere $2 million. Divided by the 6.6 million shares outstanding, that came to a tiny 31 cents a share, down to less than half of the preceding year's 79 cents. But, just look at the cash generated by Forest. Cash flow in 1980 was $44.9 million. Even the trend of cash flow was different than that of earnings. It was *up*, not down, and by 13% over the 1979 cash flow more in keeping with the increase in volume. Cash flow was $6.80, a completely different picture of the health and earning power of the company than the pitiful 31 cents in reported earnings. The practical benefits of the cash flow versus earnings should pay off in the future, because it is the backbone of the program for future expansion. During 1980, the cash flow helped to finance a capital expenditure program of over $103 million, and for 1981, the company plans to spend $150 million on its exploration and development program.

Most industrial companies won't show nearly as large a spread between their cash flows and their earnings. But they still deserve a good hard look. In particular, you can get a good feeling about how a company is actually doing by examining the details of the increases or decreases in the working capital. For example, if capital expenditures have been increased sharply, it's worth finding out why. Large plus figures for new plant and equipment, especially if the company in question has also spent a great deal on research, may be a sign that something interesting enough to get the Board of Directors to agree to spend a large amount of new money has been developed. Another thing to look for is an early sign of financial health which might be indicated by large increases in working capital, or a substantial decrease in short-term debt. On the negative side, a sharp increase in debt might indicate early signs of trouble ahead, particularly if the working capital as a whole has decreased.

Enlist the Aid of Brokers

Unfortunately, there is much factual evidence to look at. But it isn't really as difficult to get at as it may seem. Many brokerage firms have research departments that look at some of the indicators, and you can find those you want with a little effort. The price–earnings multiples are the most commonly followed, and most firms have computer runs of a number of the factors you should be looking at. The same holds for cash flow analyses. There are fewer firms which bother much about looking for stocks that are undervalued based on their asset value. But you *can* find some. E. Michael Metz and Norman Weinger at Oppenheimer & Co. are among those who do excellent work in this kind of analysis. It's not the easiest job in the world to get the sources of information you are going to want. But, it will take much less of your time and energy than worrying yourself sick about the financial crisis.

CHAPTER 8

Making Money in the Put and Call Market

During the first two weeks of March 1981 the options market had a field day. It was all due to take-over bids for three major natural resources companies. The fireworks began with Standard Oil of California's offering to buy AMAX for $78.50 per share, over double the $38 at which the stock had been trading. The SOCAL offer was the largest up until that time in United States history, totaling some $4 billion, but it shouldn't have been a complete surprise. After all, SOCAL already owned 20% of AMAX. Still, the price was so far above the market that the stock soared. But the real fireworks was in the Put and Call options market. (A *call* is an option to buy 100 shares of stock at a predetermined price at any time until its expiration date, while a *put* is an option to sell 100 shares of stock at a predetermined price at any time until its expiration date.) Call options to buy the stock at 45, expiring on March 21, only a few weeks away, skyrocketted from ¼ to 13¼. Since each call is an option to buy 100 shares of stock, it meant that anyone lucky enough to have put up $25 for a call could have cashed it in for $1325 the next day (all figures ignore commissions, which are comparatively high). It sounds like winning the sweepstakes, doesn't it? But that wasn't the end of it. Early the following week, Seagrams made an almost equally spectacular offer for St. Joe Minerals and before most options traders could catch their breaths, SOHIO bid $62 a share for Kennecott, far above the stock's last selling price of $27. The March 25 calls boomed from ⅛ to 19¼, topping the performance of the AMAX calls. As one old hand in the options business put it, "AMAX was a million to 1 shot. And we had three of them in a row."

All things considered, it was wonderful advertising for the options business. Millions of dollars were made on an investment of a few tens of thousands within a matter of only a very few days. Even more inviting from the investors point of view was the fact that the heavy losses weren't sustained by the public. It was mainly the option trading professionals who thought that a short sale of the calls with an exercise price well above the market and only a few weeks to run seemed a lead-pipe cinch to make a few bucks. Their losses were reported to be dramatic and, naturally, they called for immediate investigations as to whether there was inside knowledge of the take-over bids on the part of the buyers of the calls so that they could sue to get some of their money back. Nevertheless, for those who like the spectacle of getting the biggest possible bang for the buck, the options gave a perfect demonstration of the fact that it is the best game in town.

That doesn't please the SEC particularly. The bureaucrats are worried about the idea that options can make you rich in a hurry. They feel that it can also make for wild speculation, and are afraid that Aunt Minnie from Duluth (the synonym for the totally innocent investor) will take all of the money she received from her husband's life insurance and lose it in the options market. Of course, that is very unlikely to happen in practice. Besides, there isn't any way in which bureaucrats have ever been able to prevent gamblers from gambling. The desire of the regulators to stop a handful of occurrences could have prevented a market that is very valuable for all types of investors from becoming available to them.

Luckily, it didn't. Puts and calls had been around for a long time. In fact, there was reference to them way back in the seventeenth century. As the stock market in the United States developed wide public interest in the 1920s, a moderately sizeable options market sprung up in over-the-counter dealing. As with so many other things connected with the 1929 stock market, they were sometimes used in some rather gamey ways. The SEC couldn't forget that, so it continued to have a tongue-clucking attitude toward the put and call market right through the 1960s and into the 1970s, even though the swinging use of options that had been seen on occasion in the 1920s was definitely a thing of the past. In fact, by 1972, various divisions of the SEC had issued such contradictory opinions that the over-the-counter options market was in a state of confusion.

All of that changed abruptly in 1973 when the SEC allowed the Chicago Board to initiate buying and selling of *call* options on a newly created securities exchange. There are some cynics who are sure that the SEC allowed the new Exchange to open its doors only because the stock market was in sad enough shape to give it reason to hope that the call market would simply fade into the woodwork of inactivity. If so, the pressure to act more favorably about options would be lifted from the backs of the SEC bureaucrats. Nothing could have been further from the truth. Much to almost everyone's surprise, the Chicago Board Options Exchange became one of the biggest success stories of the 1970s. In fact, it wasn't long before the Philadelphia, Pacific, and American Exchanges wanted to get into the act. By now all of them have active options markets and the list of stocks on which there are options has grown from the original handful to a very large one. In addition to the much expanded list of calls, you can also trade put options on a number of stocks and the list of both puts and calls is continually growing. In fact, the only limitation to further expansion is the paperwork which has so swamped the Exchanges. By now it should be clear to even the worst of the original critics that the options market serves a number of investment purposes from the most speculative to the downright conservative.

The concept which allowed the options market to function so successfully owes much to the creative imagination and dogged determination of Joe Sullivan and Leo Pomerantz, the first President and Chairman of the CBOE. Before the existence of the Exchange, over-the-counter options were sold on a case-by-case basis. Meaning that if you wanted a call on XYZ, your broker would get in touch with a specialized put and call broker and arrange to buy one for you. They generally expired 30, 60, 90, or 180 days from the time of the trade. They were priced exactly at the market at the time, right down to the nearest one-eighth of a point. Clearly, options like that had virtually no secondary market. In fact, if you wanted to sell them before their expiration date, you had to take a discount. There is still some trading in those old-fashioned kinds of options, particularly for stocks that are a little off the beaten path and haven't got enough public interest to warrant being listed on one of the options exchanges. But, they don't amount to a hill of beans compared to the trading on the exchanges, or even that in the over-the-counter markets that conform their terms to those of the exchanges.

Listed Options Trading

This method of simplifying options trading and improving the secondary market was a stroke of genius pushed along by Sullivan and Pomerantz. The calls that they introduced to the Chicago Board had uniform expiration dates and uniform prices. So the secondary market became just as good as that for the stocks themselves.

In order to allow those who wanted to trade options to pick the approximate length of time they wanted, options were dated to expire on the Saturday morning after the third Friday of the month three, six, or nine months in the future. The prices are set at round numbers (5 points apart for most stocks, 10 points apart for the few higher priced ones). In that way, option buyers or sellers have a wide variety of choices about time periods and prices. The options they buy or sell can be repurchased or resold because they continue to have the same price and expiration date for their entire life. That seemingly simple change was enough to pull the options market out of a rather quiet esoteric state and to propel it into a vehicle which supports a major amount of volume. It made possible strategies which are so complicated that many of them need a computer to work them out.

Some Definitions

As mentioned briefly, a *call* is an option to buy 100 shares of stock at a predetermined price at any time until its expiration date. For instance, the call on AMAX we discussed earlier was an option to buy 100 shares at 45 good until the 21 of March, an expiration date less than a month from the time the SOCAL offer was announced. A *put* is the mirror image of that—an option to sell 100 shares of stock at a predetermined price at any time until its expiration date. The AMAX 45 March put gave the right to sell 100 shares of the stock at $45, also until March 21. In spite of these rather esoteric names, options are quite familiar to any of us who have ever taken or given them to buy a house or a car or other big-ticket items. They've been around for a long time. But until 1973, the put and call market was an over-the-counter market and generated a minor amount of volume compared to the present very active trading.

In order to make puts and calls as uniform as possible, The Options Clearing Corporation is on the other side of all trades and guarantees them. It makes sure that the brokerage firms that trade on the exchanges have the proper margin, and performs the necessary functions of policing. Times of expiration are uniform. To keep as much variety as possible, there are three cycles. Some stocks are assigned January-April-July-October dates; others February-May-August-November dates; still others March-June-September-December cycles. That explains the overlong and rather complicated listings in the newspapers. When you decide to trade in options it will become simpler than it looks at first glance, since you can follow your holdings by knowing the exchange on which it trades and the expiration date of your put or call.

Prices at which the option may be exercised, often known as the striking prices, are also kept uniform. At the expiration date of any option, a new series coming due in approximately nine months is initiated. Meanwhile, those options previously initiated are still open for trading. For example, on the day following the expiration of the January options, trading in options expiring in the following October will be opened and those expiring in April and July will still be trading. At that point, you have your choice between 3-, 6-, or 9-month options. Naturally, as the days pass, the expiration dates grow closer until the nearest one actually becomes a 1-day option.

Prices are also uniformly set. For stock selling under 100, the exercise (or striking) prices are generally fixed at 5-point intervals; over 100, they are at 10-point intervals; and over 200, they are at 20-point intervals. When trading is introduced in a new expiration month, two or three standard prices surrounding the current market price are generally selected. For example, if the underlying security trades at 37 during the period when prices are being set, the two new series of options would normally be introduced with striking prices of 35 and 40. In the case of a fast moving stock, new exercise prices may be introduced, so as to always have options outstanding with prices approximating the current market of the underlying security. Occasionally, you'll see some exercise prices at odd figures; that can occur when there is a large stock dividend. Options do not get credit of cash dividends, but they do reflect stock splits or stock dividends.

Since most stocks aren't accommodating enough to trade at the round-number intervals established by the exchanges, there is almost always a spread between the price of the stock and the exercise price of the option. For example, a June 60 IBM call representing the right to buy IBM at 60 might be selling at 6⅝ at the time when the stock itself is priced at 63⅜. Just to continue with a few terms commonly used in the options business: the 60 IBM call is said to be *in the money* since the stock is selling 3⅜ over the exercise price and could immediately be cashed in for that amount. Anyone buying the call will be paying a *premium* over the in-the-money value of 3¼ (the difference between the 6⅝ selling price of the call and the 3⅜ in-the-money points).

At the same time, there is a IBM June 70 call outstanding. That call is *out of the money* by 6⅝ points (the difference between the exercise price and the 63⅜ selling price of the stock). Even though the call would lose money if it were exercised immediately, it still commands a premium of, let's say, 2. It is quite typical that the premiums for out-of-the-money calls seem much higher than those for in-the-money calls. Take the case of a U.S. Steel July 20 option at the time that the stock sold at 31. The call sold at 11½, only a half-point premium over its in-the-money value. Meanwhile, the July 30s were selling at 3½, a 2½-point premium. Puts are the mirror images of calls, since they represent the right to sell rather than to buy the underlying stock at the pre-arranged price. Expiration dates and striking prices are handled in exactly the same way as calls.

The definitions we've been wading through may be something of a bore, but you'll have to know the language if you are going to trade in the options business. Otherwise, your broker is likely to feel as though he's speaking a foreign language. Now, we can discuss the strategies to use in dealing in options. Just to give you an idea of how complex some of the strategies can be, take a look at a fast moving stock like Teledyne. In mid-March 1981 there were no less than eight different striking prices outstanding, ranging from 140 to 220. Each of them had the usual three expiration dates—April, July, and October. In addition, there were eight puts being traded. With that many possible combinations, it's no wonder that so many professional option traders feel that they must have a computer program to point out which of the prices may get out of line and which options represent the best values.

There are three different factors that make up the value of an option. First, there's the amount that it is in the money. Second, there's the interest rate value. Since an option costs much less than the stock itself, the choice between whether to buy 100 shares of stock or an option on 100 shares depends partly on the value of the money you have to employ. For example, if you buy 100 shares of IBM at 63⅜, you'll have to put up $6337.50. If the money is worth 15%, the cost to carry the stock for 4 months would be $316.37. If call for four months can be bought at 6⅝, the interest cost would be only $33.125. In other words, you would be saving $283 in interest costs. In addition, the option is 3⅜ points in the money. Adding the intrinsic in-the-money value to the interest saving, you get $620, only $42 below the actual selling price of the call. $42 is not much to pay for the limitation of risk that you get from owning the call rather than the stock. The market can break wide open. IBM could have gone back to its year's low of 50⅜ or even below that. But all you can lose on the option is the $662.50 you've paid for it. So, the third value of an option is its insurance against a loss that exceeds the value of the option.

There's one other factor that goes into the appraisal of an option, but it's a relative value rather than one which can be as clearly determined as the other three. That's the time value. Clearly, the longer an option has to run until its expiration date, the more it is worth. Almost anyone would pay more for a 2- or 3-year call than for a 1-month call, simply because anything can happen in the future. Let's take a look at the IBM 60s as they appeared back on March 13, 1981. Calls expiring in April sold at 4½. For those expiring in July, 3 months later, the price was only 2⅛ points higher. For those expiring in October another 2½ points were added, to bring the selling price up to 8⅞. Those additions of time cost just a little above a 13% interest rate, well below the prime rate at the time which stood at a bit above 17%. The extra time was clearly a bargain from an interest rate point of view. As the exercise price gets further from the market, the premium for the extra time tends to decline, so that it is sometimes possible to create a 3-month call for only a few dollars, although it will most likely be far out of the money, and you'll need the price of the stock to reach very high levels to make a large profit. For instance, the IBM July 75s sold at ⅞, only ¾ of a point above the April's which sold for ⅛.

So, to get a good idea of what an option is worth, you should compile a table.

Cost	Intrinsic value (in or out of the money)	Interest cost of buying stock over that of the option	Insurance premium paid
6⅝	3⅜	$283	$42

Strategy 1: Buying calls or puts

Buy a call if you think the stock is going up. Obviously, anything that is true for calls is also true for puts provided you think that a stock is going down. Remember that this is a speculative strategy. If you are wrong you can lose the entire premium you've paid by the time the expiration date comes around. So, by all means don't buy options that are too short-termed. Give yourself enough time so that if the market has temporary push in the wrong direction, your position can still make a recovery. *Buy options with time to run.* Generally the extra time costs comparatively little. I always prefer the 6- or 9-month periods, because they not only provide time for my ideas to work out, but they leave room for maneuverability. There are several kinds of factors that could make you want to buy puts or calls. (1) A decision about the market in general. If you think that the recession is going to push the market down sharply, buy puts. On the other hand, when the market has been pretty well washed out, its time to start accumulating a portfolio of long-term calls. (2) It's always individual stocks you deal with. There are always some special buys if you are alert. For instance, after the AMAX, St. Joe, and Kennecott deals were announced back to back, buying calls in Newmont or Phelps Dodge or other mining companies made a great deal of sense for a short-term move. When there is a solid reason for buying a call, you don't have to be too finicky about the valuation. Just buy provided the price is at all sensible, but make sure that you limit your risk to an amount that you are prepared to lose. What's more, make sure that you don't overstay the market. One of the most common of the errors in the options business has been made by those who wait for the expiration date rather than cashing in when they have a nice profit, ignoring the further time that the option has to run. After all, there's nothing magical about those Saturday-after-the-third Friday expiration dates. (3) When you are buying puts or calls because of your feeling about the general market, stop to think about what areas will be likely to show the greatest strengths or weaknesses. After you've picked out the areas, then select the stocks. Part of your selection process should take into account the value of the option, for which you can use the preceding table. You should be able to combine a reasonably priced option with a stock that fits in with your market strategy. Remember to allow yourself enough time so that if your market judgment isn't immediately justified, you can get a second chance.

Strategy 2: The Straddle

There are times when it's difficult to tell just what is going to happen to the market except that which ever way it moves, it should be large-scale. Such times are usually either when the market is in terrible shape and everyone is bearish or when the market is doing very well because the majority is quite bullish. Options offer a way to take advantage of very large moves by owning a combination of a put and a call on *the same stock* commonly known as a straddle. For example, with IBM's stock selling at 63⅜, you might have purchased a call at 60 with an expiration date about 4 months away for 6⅝, and at the same time you might have bought a put at 60 for 2⅛. With an investment of 8¾ points, you would be in a position to wait for fluctuation in the price of the stock. Since the call is in the money by 3⅜, you need an upward move of 5⅜ to pay for both options. On the other hand, the put is out of the money by the same 3⅜ so you'd need a plunge of over 12 points in the stock to pay for your options. Since the range of the stock for the year was 22⅜ points—with a low of 50⅜ and a high of 72¾—such moves would not be extraordinary. If IBM breaks below 51¾ or above 68¾, you start to make money. What's more, you have time to change your mind. If the market tumbles and it seems ready for a recovery, you can sell out your put, pocket the profit and hang on to the call. If IBM rallies sharply enough to seem ready for a correction, you can sell your call and wait. Once again, you have the chance to calculate the exact extent of your loss if the market doesn't move much one way or the other in the 4 months until the options expire. You can't get hit for more than your investment in the straddles.

Strategy 3: Spreads

With so many options at different prices and different time periods, it is possible to take on a number of kinds of positions which can limit your risk and still provide for a very healthy return on your money.

Point spread: Buy an IBM July 60 call at 6⅝ and sell short an IBM 70 at 2. If the stock should go to 70 or higher, you would make 10 points on the call you own—the difference between your exercise price of 60 and the exercise price of 70, at which you are short. Your cost would be 4⅝—the difference between the 6⅝ you paid for the call and the 2 you received for the one that you sold short. In other words, you would have made 5⅜ on a 4⅝ investment—over 100% on your money in 4 months. Your risk is that the stock will sell for below 64⅝, so that the call which you are long will not make enough to pay back your cost. In fact, if IBM sells below 60, you will lose your entire 4⅝ investment. The strategy is, therefore, a bullish one. If you are bearish, you might do a similar spread on IBM puts. Buy an IBM July 70 put for 7¼ and sell a July 60 short at 2⅛. Your investment is 5⅛ points. If IBM sells at 60 or below, you will make 4⅞ on the investment (the 10 points of the spread between 70 and 60 minus the 5⅛ point cost). It's not quite 100% on your money, but it's close to it and in only 4 months. Your risk is that IBM will sell above 64⅞ by expiration date and if you are wrong and IBM sells at 70 or above, you'll lose your entire 5⅛ investment.

These point spread strategies are usually double or nothing affairs. The spread should be about double the amount of your investment at the outset. There are better strategies and, of course, it is always possible to lower your investment and increase your potential return by selling more than one call or put. It will increase your risk if the stock goes up or down too much, so you will have to put pencil and paper to the calculations of your possible losses, but it is a perfectly good technique to employ. Remember that the strategy of spreading is a very complicated and if you wish to pursue it, try to find a broker with access to a computer program that can pick out the best available spreads and even compare them with the estimated range of the stock during the time period of your involvement.

Writing (Selling) Options

The selling of options employs a completely different strategy than that of buying them. It is a strategy primarily intended to earn a return. So, clearly, any approach to the selling of options should be a careful one. The less risk the better. The best of all possible option writing programs would be to sell calls on short-term Treasury bills because you know exactly what they will be worth at maturity. Unfortunately, there's no demand for such calls. On the other side of the spectrum is the sale of calls (or puts) on a wildly speculative stock without owning it (or without being short in the case of puts). The example of Kennecott is a dramatic demonstration of just how risky that can get! Just imagine how much you could have lost by selling the Kennecott calls before the take-over deal was announced without having owned the stock! Selling calls without owning the stock is known as writing naked calls (the same term is used for selling puts without being short the stock). Naked option selling is highly speculative, and since you can't even make more than the premium you are paid, it is a strategy best left to professional investors who can follow the movements of the stocks on a minute-by-minute basis.

If you want to own (or be short, in the case of a put) the stock on which you are writing an option, you will be known as a covered option writer. You should have as your objective to make about double the prevailing interest rate by pursuing a strategy which doesn't have any extraordinary risks. The idea is that you should pick out a stock that you would be willing to own, and then to sell calls on it. If the stock goes up, the call you have written will be exercised and you will pocket the premium. It doesn't matter how high the stock goes, all you can make is the premium. But, a covered option writer is always delighted when the stock goes up, although he may feel a little twinge of regret if it goes sky-high, because he could have made more money by just owning the stock without having written a call against it. However, since the risk in covered call writing is that the stock will go down more than the amount of the premium, any upward move is always welcome. If you are very bearish, it's better to sell puts and to sell the stock short. In that way you pocket the premium if the stock goes down and have to worry only if it goes up more than the amount of the premium. Let's look at a few examples.

Strategy; Covered Call Writing

Buy 100 shares of Standard Oil of California at 40. Sell 1 September 40 call at 5. You will get the $500 call price credited to your account immediately, so your net investment is $3500. Make up a table:

Price of Stock	Call price	Money needed	Number of months
40	5	$3500	6

Dividends	Annual return	Break-even price	Annual range of stock
$1.00	34%	34	39¼–48½

The rate of 34% fits the bill of being at least double the amount of the prevailing interest rate (the prime rate at the time was 17% and 6-month certificates yielded 12.3%). In order to achieve that rate of return, you have to count in the dividends. Call options do not get credit for the dividends paid by the underlying stock, so you get to keep them. Since Standard of California paid $2 a year, you should get half a year's payout during the 6-month period of the call. But, check the dividend expiration dates carefully when you sell a call. You may be unlucky and just miss a dividend date, and that would reduce your rate of return.

Of course, option writing doesn't stop there. You'll get a 34% rate of return (minus commissions) provided the stock stays above 40. It doesn't matter how high the stock goes because you must part with it at 40 and your profit will be limited to the $5 premium, plus the dividend. But, suppose the stock declines instead? If it breaks 40, you will have a loss. You have 6 points to protect you against that loss, so you won't lose unless the stock breaks to 34. Since the stock's low for the year was 39½ versus a high of 48½, that's not such a bad protection point. But, sometimes the stock options you write *will* go down, giving you less of a return than your original calculation, or even an actual loss. So you must reduce your expectations of the possible return from an option writing strategy. A good rule of thumb is to reduce the original premium percentage realization by approximately 30% to take possible losses into consideration. I've never met an option writer who didn't sustain some losses, so don't be carried away by promises of sensational returns. You can earn a very satisfactory return on your money, substantially in excess of bank rates, and most likely better than the Dow Jones and Standard and Poor's Averages which are so often used as the measuring stick of proper performance. But, you must be careful and avoid bad declines in the market. It's best to write options when the market is in a gradual and long-lived upturn (or downturn, if you are a put writer).

If you are a put writer because of your expectation of a bear market, you will usually get a little less than you will for calls, but it is a strategy which can earn money in a bear market just when everyone else is losing. It is a safer, although perhaps not as profitable, way as selling short because you are protected by the amount of the premium.

A final option writing strategy is to sell a straddle—a put and a call, both at the same price expiring on the same date.

The advantage is that the psychology of the stock market usually keeps the buyers from exercising their puts or calls until sometime close to the expiration date. Most of the time the stock is either far enough up or down so that only one side of the straddle either the put or the call will be exercised. So, you have a much larger premium to work with. In the case of Standard Oil of California, the September 40 put sold at 3½. Add that to the price of the call, and your total premium would now be 8½ points. If you feel that SOCAL will advance, you may well regard the extra premium (and percentage you can make) as found money. But watch it! If you are wrong and SOCAL goes down, you will be put with an extra 100 shares of stock. That, of course, increases your risk. Some old hands at option writing decide to take that risk into consideration by buying less than the amount of stock needed to cover their call options (say, 50 shares for each call instead of the 100 required for full coverage). That way, if the stock declines and they get put with another hundred shares, they will have the 8¼ points premium to protect themselves against a position of 150 shares rather than 200. When that sort of thing happens, the technique they usually employ is to sell new options on the 150 shares they will wind up with. Straddles increase the potential yield, but they also increase the risk.

Conclusion and General Recommendation

Options are undoubtedly more complicated than most aspects of the securities business. But, they present wonderful opportunities for anyone with a conviction to make a very large percentage on his money if he is right. So, you should limit the amount of money you invest to a sum that you can afford to lose.

As the recession deepens, a small portfolio of puts makes quite a bit of sense. Later on, when the Reagan Administration begins to try its best to save the economy, switch into calls. Option writers should wait until after the severity and duration of the recession is clearer than it is at present.

CHAPTER 9

The Way Out

When you compare the change in the status of the United States since the end of World War II, you receive quite a nasty shock. In 1946, we reigned supreme in the world. We were not only well-loved by most of the world, but we were clearly the main hope for its industrial well-being. Our dollar was the only trustworthy currency and it was up to us to rebuild the broken-down machinery of world commerce and production. We *did* accomplish remarkable results, but in the process, we have declined from our top-of-the-mountain position. A billion people have learned the phrase "Yankee Go Home". The dollar is regaining some of its strength, but not until after it had been under tremendous attack. We are concerned with whether our military might is still greater than that of the Soviets. And, in a number of economic areas, including one as important as automobiles, we can no longer make claim to the "number 1" position. In fact, if you compare the broad view of the present to that of 35 years ago, you get the eerie feeling that you've been reading one of the chapters of the *Decline and Fall of the Roman Empire.*

Gloomy as this downward progression may seem, it can be reversed provided we understand why it happened and what must be done to correct it.

Reason for Our Decline

Part of the declining process was natural enough. After all, at the end of World War II we were unreasonably powerful. Most of the productive capacity of the world had been either destroyed or exhausted by the war. Instead of taking advantage of that, we chose to help both for political and humanitarian reasons. After the Marshall plan and the rebuilding of Germany and Japan (which ultimately came from the pockets of our taxpayers), there was no way in which we could remain uniquely powerful in the industrial sense. In fact, the reverse was true. Western Europe and Japan replaced their destroyed industry with new plants, many of them far more efficient than ours. The dollars which we spent so generously found their way into hoards by both individuals and central banks, only to be thrown out as an oversupply when the slightest weakness in our structure became evident.

However, in addition to that normal weakening of power, there was the nastier part that came from our own mistakes. They really began to accumulate during the mid-1960s with the Vietnam War. The outpouring of our political and economic resources without paying for them as we went allowed other countries to steal a march on us industrially. It set the stage for a difficult-to-control inflation rate, and the fight against it kept our new plant and equipment expenditures at a low level for many years. Finally, it allowed aggressive elements in the world to feel that if the Viet Cong could tweak Uncle Sam's beard, so could they.

Perhaps Presidents Nixon, Ford, and Carter can be forgiven for not realizing that the United States faced such difficult long-term problems. After all, when you are the greatest, it's difficult to realize that you are losing some of your power. Still, there's no question that they complicated and increased our problems by trying to solve short-term difficulties as they came up rather than by taking aim at the long term. That spit-and-polish series of actions by all three Presidents simply put us into worse shape.

Fortunately for us, President Reagan seems to be ready to tackle the long-term problems regardless of the political cost. He's got quite a job on his hands, and it will become worse as he faces the depth of the recession. But if he stands firm, the problems themselves are likely to bring about their own solutions, if only they are allowed the freedom to do so. Let's take a look at the main problems.

Our Main Problems

We've tried to avoid the need for a guns-and-butter economy ever since the end of the Vietnam War by de-emphasizing our military, but our approach to the Soviet Union has failed to produce any real attempt at disarmament. In fact, it had the opposite effect. The Soviets have escalated their defense expenditures until they have exceeded ours by a huge amount. The strain on the Communist empire is beginning to show. Countries behind the Iron Curtain are having serious difficulties keeping their consumers in line. It may be that our new tough stance and heavily increased defense expenditures will turn out to be a very clever move in the geopolitical chess game. The Russians may not be able to afford to keep up with us without facing insuperable consumer revolts. But, in the meantime, we cannot afford guns *and* butter either. In our case, butter is defined as social services rather than food itself. We have to give up enough of our social welfare system to pay for our increased military spending. There's every indication that President Reagan is ready to do that, and there's a good chance that he can carry Congress along with him. If he doesn't it will simply mean a recurrence of the Vietnam mistake of not paying-as-you-go, and the Federal debt will get even further out of hand.

The old structure of the world has been changed by OPEC. It's not only oil prices that have altered the ability of industrialized countries to cope, but it's the growing awarness by other countries whose principal resources are raw materials that they will try the same kind of cartelization as soon as they get the chance. The giant oil companies know more about the effect of international cartels than anyone else. After all, they have been the ones which have had to cope most directly with OPEC. They have made the clearest prediction of what they expect to happen to raw materials prices over the next decade by the way in which they have been gobbling up natural resources companies. Just look at the bids for St. Joe, Kennecott, and AMAX at prices far exceeding those on the stock market before their moves.

The future potential is obvious. No longer will raw materials be available cheaply while those who turn them into useful objects profit greatly. The time has come when raw material producing nations will be sharing the wealth. That places a premium on the efficiency of the manufacturing process. That's where the United States has been lagging sadly behind. In the 1970s, we invested only 10.2% of our Gross National Product in new plants and equipments, as opposed to 12.6% by West Germany, and 17% by Japan. As a result, the average age of our plants and equipment is 16-17 years, as opposed to 12 years for that of West Germany, and 10 years for that of Japan. Those figures take on an even grimmer look when you consider how fast technology has been moving in recent years. Our need is very clear. We must start massive capital spending. To do that, we must reverse the continual tittilation of the consumer which has been so attractive to our last three Presidents. The belts of our consumers must be tightened to make it possible to renovate our industrial structure. So far, President Reagan's plans in that direction aren't quite as convincing as they might be, but we won't really know the answers until the recession is nearer to its bottom. That will be the time to resist all calls to restimulate consumption and to concentrate on the slower path of rebuilding our plants and equipment. If the President is going to be able to do that, he'll have to convince businessmen that he will stick to his guns throughout his entire administration.

The debt structure must be reoriented. There's just too much emphasis on short-term credit. The result has been a huge outpouring into money market funds, while the United States Treasury so dominates the long-term and intermediate debt market that financing the development of new industrialization is very difficult. To accomplish our purpose, interest rates for long-term debt must decline to the point where the stock market can be strong enough to take on its traditional function of financing true risk ventures, while the long-term bond market can be counted on to finance a renewed drive toward the re-equipment of our major corporations. The Federal debt must be reduced enough so that long-term bonds will once more become attractive enough to such enforced savers as insurance companies and pension funds. The easiest way to do that is to reduce inflationary expectations, which will automatically improve the bond market. That is most likely to be accomplished by the recession we are now experiencing.

Serious as these problems are, they also carry the potentials of their own solutions, particularly if the Federal authorities resist spit-and-polish solutions.

The Solutions

Our military build-up should not have as big an effect as escalations we have seen in actual times of war. The reason is that there will be a large concentration on highly sophisticated weaponry which costs a great deal, but doesn't require any huge quantities of our basic industrial production. If military expenditures are offset by a drop in consumer spending, which has a larger multiplier effect on the economy, inflation can actually be decreased even with an arms build-up. In the meantime, at least some of strength in the economy will be preserved. That may not help ease the recession, but it should provide an area in which intelligent investors can function.

The greatest immediate problem we face is still energy, in spite of an increasingly relaxed attitude caused by the present oversupply. While it is true that everyone who can is looking for more oil and natural gas (the number of drilling rigs in operation in the United States is down somewhat, but still near a record high level), and there is a large amount of money being spent on the search for alternate sources, neither is likely to turn out to be the main push of our industry. That will most likely come from methods of using energy more efficiently, so that we will need less energy to give us the same amount of power. It won't be a cheap process, and if it weren't for the unconscionable increase in OPEC prices, no one would be willing to spend the required money. But, as a practical matter, it can pay both individuals and industries to invest heavily in energy saving. Some of the ways in which that can be done are the following:

Computer-controlled energy management. A move in this direction has already begun in commercial buildings. These systems can slice as much as 25% from energy bills by simply regulating inside temperature in a way which takes into account all of the heat generated by machines, lights, and people. The market for such management techniques is expected to grow at a rapid pace.

Residential energy management is a multibillion dollar market already. Consultation on how to save money on home energy bills is available in many parts of the country through local utilities and other private companies. With the benefits available for householders to ease the cost of the equipment required, this market should grow rapidly.

The use of new products such as heat pumps and energy efficient motors, analyzing and metering equipment is at the stage of rapid expansion. Exxon may have made a mistake in its acquisition of Reliance Electric if it thought that it had a highly efficient electrical motor almost ready for the market, but the fact that it made as large an investment as it did speaks volumes for the future of the industry.

Co-generation is still a market that commands under $1 billion in sales. But, with the cost of energy having skyrocketed, what could be more natural than the desire not to waste it? The same unit of oil, gas, or coal can be used in several different ways. The most natural idea is to avoid wasting the steam which was so often simply allowed to vanish into thin air when fuel costs were low. A law passed in 1978 requires that the local utilities buy excess power from industrial generators. All things considered, the market for co-generation equipment could increase by some 20-fold over the next decade.

Burning waste products to generate energy or steam has been discussed for years, but it has had technical difficulties to solve. Many of the problems are now past history, and the industry is poised to take off.

Solar energy has seen only limited use. But, a considerable amount of progress has been made not only in the heating of water, but in the powering of such large complexes as that in the State capitol building in Sacramento, California. The next step, just in the beginning stages, is the commercial use of solar cells to generate energy economically. This could be a huge industry once it gets started.

The amount of dollars that will be spent on saving energy is astronomical. The Mellon Institute, for example, expects that between now and the end of the century over $350 billion will be spent on improving automobile fuel efficiency, about $250 billion more on installing fuel-to-energy conversion equipment, and $100 billion to provide residences with proper insulation. Add to that the amount which will be spent on the search for oil and natural gas, and the extra billions which will be put into alternate sources of energy. Don't forget that none of that includes what would happen if there is the almost inevitable breakthrough into solar or some other form of power. It all adds up to this: we have an enormous new program to bolster our industrial progress and one which is important enough for our society to receive the support of all but some of the lunatic fringes. It will start slowly, but by a few years from now it should be important enough to give our overall business picture a tremendous boost.

So, the economic blueprint for the future of the United States is clear-cut. First, we must unburden ourselves of many of our past mistakes and some nonmistakes that are simply outmoded. That will be a painful process, especially since we will also be struggling with disinflation. It's a combination that makes a deep recession inevitable. But unlike the early 1930s, our economic hero is ready to save us.

The economic hero (or rather the four heroes) are, in order of their appearance, the following:

Rapidly escalating defense expenditures. That's not enough to pull us out of the recession all by itself, but it's a big help.

A tax cut to rescue consumption. That will take some time to develop—much more than the Reagan Administration hopes. But, sooner or later, it can join forces with the other three.

A new upward push in plant and equipment spending, probably starting sometime in 1983, after large corporations become accustomed to disinflation, and begin to get more secure about their cash generation.

Spending for energy, which will start slowly and then gain momentum.

It is a powerful new structure to look forward to—provided the Reagan Administration doesn't become alarmed by the fact that the recession will last too long for comfort. It has every promise of putting the United States back in its world-leading economic role. In fact, we are already getting an indication of that from the strength of the dollar.

It's almost a perfect scenario for making money in the security markets. First, the recession should make plenty of buying opportunities. Then, as the recession bottoms out, the market should be on the rise. It should easily top all previous highs, and the Dow Jones Industrial Average should be over 2000 by 1984 or 1985.

The Stocks to Buy

Of course, there can be reasons for any stock to be attractive. But, in general, I would be looking for companies in nine broad industrial groups for my future investments. The first five groups are those that should be off and running once the downward force of the economy eases a bit—if, in fact, they are damaged by it at all. The other four groups are for bargain hunting. I've referred to some of these nine areas previously, but I would like to list them all together in a more organized way.

Defense. The Government will be spending a fortune in this area for the foreseeable future. But, the best candidates for investment are likely to be some of the smaller companies rather than the giants with huge, highly publicized contracts. Any of those big missile or aircraft programs can run into political pressure or delays which can create cost problems. On the other hand, those companies which make highly sophisticated gear that improves the efficiency of our armed forces are more apt to be free of politics or changing military procurement plans. There are plenty of those to choose from.

Alternate energy. Solar energy is still not cost-efficient, but there are a number of companies which are trying hard to make it competitive, and some of them will probably succeed. Even with the price of oil down from its high, it's still too expensive to use as we did ten years ago, when it cost only $2.10 a barrel. Companies that make products which will conserve energy or develop methods of using it more efficiently will find good markets for their products, even in a weak economy. That also holds true for those who can improve production from oil and natural gas wells.

Medical. People always will require medical treatment, no matter how the economy performs; and some means or other will be found to pay their expenses. But there will be a drive to increase the efficiency of providing health services. New methods of preparing drugs, wider distribution of generic products, and tools to improve some of the antiquated methods of medical service will lay the groundwork for a more dynamic industry. Obviously, there will be miracle drugs, but it is impossible to predict which companies will develop them. Gene-splitting is an exciting new field, but it is a good idea to choose those companies that actually have some commercial products rather than those which are engaged solely in paid research.

Robots and computer-controlled tools. Once capital spending begins to increase, these products should really take off. Japan is already a leader in the field, but American technology certainly won't take a back seat. Can there be a better way to improve productivity than to have as many manufacturing processes as possible become completely automated?

High technology. Once again, there's a great deal of publicity concerning the Japanese take-over a large share of the market. But with the military using a good many high-technology products, and with the boost that they can give to productivity in offices as well as in factories, the companies that make them should be off to a fast start once there's the first indication of an easing of the recession.

Bargain Hunting

Stocks in this group are unusually depressed because they are in businesses that are suffering from the economic slump. They can be excellent buys just because they *are* suffering. But, you must be sure that their financial structure is good enough to withstand any present adversity, so that they can be around to take advantage of the eventual upswing.

Oil and natural gas. The glut of oil won't last indefinitely. In addition, even with a further decrease in the price, the value of the reserves in the ground of many companies is far greater than the selling prices of their stock. Besides, natural gas will be gradually de-controlled. It all leads to the probability that balance sheet analysis will really pay off. Shares of the giant oil companies may be good investments, but the real play will be in the medium-sized oil and natural gas companies that are selling for well below their value. Even the Canadian companies deserve an examination. They've been terribly battered by the destructive Canadian energy policy, but eventually companies find a way to cope, no matter how many obstacles governments put in their way.

Oil services. The number of drilling rigs in use has declined from the record level of 1981, and with it the demand for oil field supplies has slackened. But, it's still very profitable to hit a successful well, and it's nice to increase domestic production. Companies that conduct seismographic surveys and supply equipment for drilling or producing oil and gas should have good post-recession prospects. When their stocks become cheap enough, they should be worth buying.

Housing. This *really* is a bargain hunting area. Obviously, housing starts will improve some day. When they do, there will be new, more efficient building methods. Companies that are in the forefront of new construction techniques, and that are strong enough to survive the current slump, should be able to provide large gains for those who have enough courage to buy them when no one else wants them.

Conglomerates. They are a group of stocks that are just made to order for balance sheet analysis. The stock of many of these companies are selling at prices that are reminiscent of the days of Ben Graham. Be sure that those in which you want to invest are profitable, so that the asset values won't be wiped out by large losses or write-offs.

So, there's the prescription for making money in the disinflation. First, get together some cash and invest in long- or intermediate-term bonds, or even in some of the more speculative areas of the bond market. Then, form your buying program for stocks. Start slowly, but keep in mind the idea that you will pyramid your investments as the economic blueprint of recovery becomes an actual structure.

Index

Acquisitions, 129
Allen, Charles, 142
Alternate energy stocks, 178
AMAX, 155, 156, 159, 173
American Hawaiian Steamship
    Company, 126
Arab Emirates, 52
Art and antique acutions, 28
Art and Auction Magazine, 28

Balance sheet analysis, 121-127
Bank of the United States, 69-71
Banking system, 9, 10
Barron's, 119
Biddle, Nicholas, 67, 70, 71
Black Death. *See* Bubonic Plague
Bolingbroke (Henry IV, English
    King), 45
Bond Market, 90-97, 103, 174
    future of, 96
    futures in, 110-112
    history of, 96-97
    investing in, 103-113
    speculating in, 109-110
    transformation of, 97-98
Bonds, corporate, 106-107
    deep discount, 108
    government agency, 106
    long-term government, 91
    "swapping" of, 97-98
    treasury, 105
    valuation of, 90-91
Brokers, 154, selection of, 119
Bubonic Plague, 41-46, 66, economic
    and social effects of, 43-46
Burns, Arthur, 3, 17, 139-140
Business Week, 119
Business slumps, characteristics of,
    86-89

Calls, 155-161
    buying of, 162, 163-164
    covered, 166, 167-169
    definition of, 159
    in the money, 160-161

    naked, 166
    out of the money, 161
    writing, 166-169
Capital spending, 12
Carter, Jimmy, 23, 46, 47, 171
Carter Administration, 47
Cash, 89
Cash flow analysis, 150-154, of oil
    companies, 151-152
Chase, Salmon P., 73, 75, economic
    programs of, 74-76
Chicago Board of Trade, 112, 157
Chicago Board Option Exchange
    (CBOE), 157, 158
Christie's Auction Gallery, 28
Chrysler Corporation, 88
Civil War, 73-78, aftermath of, 77-80
Clemenceau, Georges, 20
Co-generation, 175-176
Commerce Department, 102
Commodities prices, 26-27
Conglomerates, 128-130, 180
Consumer Price Index, 30, 99-100
Consumer spending, 12, 13, 14
Cooke, Jay, 76, 78, 80
Corporate bond market, 106-107
Corporate bonds, 106-108, New
    wrinkles in, 107-108
Corporate borrowing, 94
Cost-push inflation. *See* Inflation,
    cost-push
Credit, 57, 88
"Crowding-out" theory, 95
Current assets, 121, 123
Current liabilities, 121, 123

Deep discount bonds, 108
Defense area, 147
Defense spending, 14
Defense stocks, 178
Demand-pull inflation. *See*
    Inflation, demand-pull
Denarius, 36, 37, silver content of, 38
Diocletian (Roman Emperor), 35-38,
    41, 66, monetary policies of,
    37-39

181